W9-AXQ-639

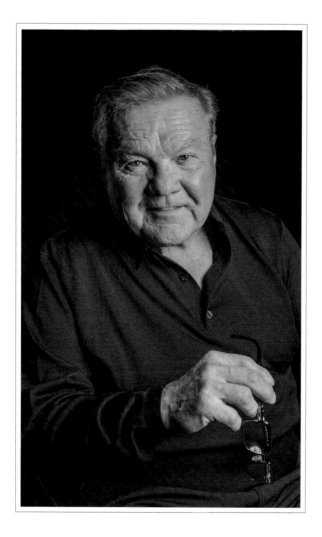

Open Secrets of Success

THE GARY THARALDSON STORY

Patrick J. McCloskey

UNIVERSITY OF MARY PRESS

© 2017 by University of Mary

Third Printing, April 2019

All rights reserved. No part of this book may be reproduced in any form without written permission of the copyright owners.

Published in the United States of America by
University of Mary Press
7500 University Drive
Bismarck, ND 58504
www.umary.edu

ISBN 978-0-9988728-5-8

Design: Jerry Anderson
Illustrations: Tom Marple & Jerry Anderson

Printed in Canada

This book is dedicated to everyone who reads it.

CONTENTS

FOREWORD

Congressman Kevin Cramer

GROWING UP in the small town of Kindred, North Dakota, I learned the same values of family, faith and hard work as did Gary Tharaldson in the even smaller town of Dazey, 90 miles away. Decades later when I worked with the Harold Schafer Leadership Foundation at the University of Mary, Gary was a frequent topic of discussion and example for our students.

When the University of Mary named its business school after him, my mother-in-law, Janet Neumann, asked me if our Gary Tharaldson was the same person who sold her mother a nursing home insurance policy in the 1970s. Janet told me how this insurance agent in Valley City was extremely attentive to her mother and her long-term care needs. As the time neared for her to need this care, Gary came to Cando to review with Janet her mother's plan. At that meeting he suggested a new product that would serve her needs even better than the one she had.

Clearly, this was the same Gary Tharaldson who taught high school in Leonard before owning his first hotel—a Super 8 in Valley City in 1982.

From there he built the largest privately owned hospitality empire in the nation, was recognized as the state's richest resident and became the subject of university leadership classes.

As he was developing his business empire, he brought his common-sense approach to projects with many partners across the United States. It was inevitable he would cross paths with another hospitality industry giant who is now the nation's chief executive. President Donald J. Trump and I have visited a few times about Gary and the joint Las Vegas project that brought them together.

Gary recognizes failures and mistakes as a reality of his many years in business. He has told me he believes failure serves a purpose. In it he sees potential, often offering a gateway to greater success. He often says the mistake many business people make is trying to sell their product to people who don't need it, rather than focusing on people who can be helped by whatever it is they are selling. Harold Schafer used to say he didn't sell cleaning products—he helped housewives clean their homes.

Gary, from Dazey, and Harold, from Stanton, have more in common than coming from small North Dakota communities. Or perhaps it is the commonality of a small Midwest town upbringing that made them both the best in their businesses. Starting with nothing in terms of financial resources, they had everything in terms of determination, a tremendous work ethic, a vivid and practical imagination and a deep dedication to community.

When I served as North Dakota's director of tourism in the mid-1990s, it was a point of pride for me that one of the world's largest hotel owners was headquartered in Fargo. I learned firsthand about Gary's generosity and sense of patriotism, as he frequently shared his resources with my team as we marketed North Dakota to the region's travelers. His sense of "thinking big" challenged us to play a bigger role in organizations such as the Old West Trail and Rocky Mountain International.

Our paths have crossed often since those days of promoting North Dakota tourism, as Gary has quietly shared his wealth with employees, schools, charities and civic projects across the state. Every one of our encounters brings the same humble Gary Tharaldson, who as a young insurance salesman put the needs of his clients ahead of the policies he was selling. This is one of the many "open secrets" that brought him and his businesses great success and admiration and gratitude from all who have been privileged to know him.

INTRODUCTION

Patrick J. McCloskey

Stick to your knitting.

Bill Marriott

IF SUCCESS HAS A SECRET, it is how to build a bridge between knowing and doing. This book's aim is to articulate the knowing and illustrate the doing in the story of Gary Tharaldson's remarkable success. Hopefully seeing how Gary built his business literally from nothing will inspire confidence in readers, especially in young men and women beginning their careers. Success is possible, but not all roads lead there.

Gary created an astonishing pathway to success in the hospitality industry. Some readers might want to follow directly in Gary's footsteps. Most others will likely wish to apply the lessons of Gary's career to aspirations in other directions.

Simply put, Gary builds and runs hotels. He has constructed more than 425 hotels to date and has 60 additional hotels at various stages of development. By decade's end he will eclipse the 500- mark. At that point, Gary might "slow down," he says with a mischievous twinkle in his hazel eyes. Gary loves his work and is now having "the time of my life."

Since the mid-1990s, Forbes Magazine has listed Gary as the richest person in North Dakota. In 1997 and 1998, he was included in the Forbes 400, the annual ranking of America's wealthiest. Forbes calculated Gary's net worth in 2016 at $980 million, which Gary said was conservative but "fairly accurate." A year later, Forbes listed his net worth at $900 million, which was puzzling since his assets had grown significantly. In the next five years, his net worth will be two to three times Forbes' estimation.

However, Gary does not hoard his wealth, nor does he pursue money making for its own sake. Instead, he uses financial resources to build companies that create thousands of good-paying jobs, provide high-quality services and benefit the communities in which he locates his hotels and other interests. He has also given away vast amounts of money to employees, family members and causes he believes in.

The word "billionaire" conveys a sense of unimaginable plenty. Only about 0.00000027 percent of people worldwide are billionaires in monetary terms at present. The proportion of super rich will not increase dramatically in the future. Nor is such bounty everyone's goal, since it comes with a heavy burden of responsibility. Heavy is the crown, and just as heavy is the gold in the crown.

However, we all aspire to live a full life, to reach lofty—for us—goals. No one would think of evaluating a teacher's career in terms of his or her salary. Most of us have had the opportunity to meet and even study under a master mentor at some point. The fabulous treasures generated by this instructor are measured in lives enriched and transformed. Just as a biography of this teacher would illustrate life lessons applicable to other careers including business, so Gary's strategies and wisdom are applicable to the success of any other career, including teaching—which is exactly where his career started.

The keys to Gary Tharaldson's enormous success are no secret. Remarkably, throughout his career, he has always told anyone who asked—including competitors—exactly how to succeed in the hospitality industry. And he has never held back any significant details, despite being highly competitive.

Since relatively few people will benefit from Gary's direct counsel, this book seeks to distill his wisdom for present and future readers. Success, of course, cannot be reduced to a set of do's and don'ts. Gary lived and continues to live by his credo, which focuses on treating customers and employees well.

"Not only do I create jobs," Gary said, "but my whole philosophy is: How do I make it better for people that work for me? How do I make them wealthy?" And Gary has fulfilled his promise: "I made people wealthy beyond their belief."

But as we all know in our business and private lives, treating others well is far from easy. In fact, failing to do so is often more common and accounts for the majority of personal tragedies, social and governmental dysfunctions, and business failures.

Seeing how Gary has fulfilled this commitment, and continues to do so in new ways, hopefully will help the reader find ways to apply the Golden Rule more acutely in his or her life.

Gary is a confident man, but not boastful and certainly not arrogant. Humble and honest come to mind immediately. Practically, he has a keen sense of what works and what doesn't, and he acts decisively. He is a builder who does not pursue profit as an end in itself. Money is an objective measure of success, but far more importantly for Gary, a necessary component of commerce. Money is the fuel that powers an enterprise and helps create a prosperous, free society. It is a substance of necessity and a foundation of liberty, but it is not an object of worship.

We can learn important lessons from Gary's failures, as well. Everybody falls down, falls short. Businessman and politician Stanley J. Randall wryly noted, "The closest to perfection a person ever comes is when he fills out a job application form." The gravity of human nature pulls hardest on those who climb highest. Ironically, just after Gary's biggest score in his lodging career, a chasm opened up between what he knew about success and how he acted. He made mistakes—huge miscalculations that endangered his investments and businesses—which he can only laugh about today, since he is well on the way to recovering completely. Hopefully, Gary's misadventures will help others avoid the same traps.

As novelist James Michener put it, "Character consists of what you do on the third and fourth tries." Business and life challenges either develop and strengthen character, or twist and destroy our humanity. Twenty-five hundred years ago, Heraclitus wrote that "[c]haracter is destiny." Peers in the hospitality industry describe Gary as "a man of great character." Integrity was essential to his success and to his ability to overcome missteps. And ultimately, character will be his legacy. Not even multibillionaires can take a penny with them.

The Greek philosopher also said, to paraphrase, that you can't step in the same river twice. On the individual level, opportunities fly by as the majority of players hesitate. Similarly, most organizations seem to be built upon the notion that you can—indeed, must, according to standard paralysis (versus operating) procedures—step in the same river twice and keep doing it regardless of the fact that the opportunity and/or necessity to act are long gone. Gary's capacity to make quick, sound decisions provides a prime example of what makes a leader great, and how a leader empowers his organization to make sound choices and remain nimble.

In accordance with Gary's straightforward personality and humble character, I refer to him by his first name throughout the book, rather than by "Tharaldson" as is customary in newspapers, magazines and books. He is a friend, whether or not you have met him.

Open Secrets of Success

THE GARY THARALDSON STORY

The Man, The Call & The Big Dilemma

A man has no more character than he
can command in a time of crisis.

Ralph W. Sockman

Only those who will risk going
too far can possibly find out
how far one can go.

T.S. Eliot

ON A SUNNY MORNING in Las Vegas in May 2012, the phone rang on Aimee Fyke's desk. Fyke is the Chief Operating Officer (COO) of Tharaldson Hospitality Management, which means she runs the operations side of all of Gary's hotels. Fyke began working for Gary 25 years ago when she was only 23.

In 1999, Gary moved his family and headquarters from Fargo to Las Vegas. At this point, he no longer owned any hotels in North Dakota or any of the surrounding states. No longer having to endure winters on the Northern Great Plains was certainly part of the attraction south. He would be able to play on his beloved softball team year-round, too.

"Aimee?" a familiar voice asked. "This is Gary."

After asking how she and her family were doing, Gary suddenly said, "I'm going to have to declare bankruptcy."

Fyke was stunned. She knew Gary had been troubled by cash flow problems since the Great Recession began in 2008. But how was bankruptcy even remotely possible? For the last 30 years, Gary had an incredible Midas touch in almost every business venture, and his mistakes were minor in comparison to his successes.

Fyke recalled that in September 2005, Gary partnered with Centex Destination Properties, a division of homebuilder Centex Corporation, to buy the Westward Ho Hotel and Casino on the Las Vegas Strip for $145.5 million. The Westward Ho, which opened in 1963, was a hotel-casino with 27 buildings—with 777 (of course) rooms—on the property. Perhaps the fact that the Westward Ho's lodging was motel-style—that is, the buildings were surrounded by parking spaces with outside entrances to the rooms—appealed subliminally to Gary. To this day he calls his hotels "motels," even though he never built or owned a motel. In fact, the Westward Ho was advertised as "The World's Largest Motel."

Centex and Gary planned to close the Westward Ho, which they did in November 2005, and then demolish the structures on the 18-acre site. The Las Vegas Review-Journal reported that Gary was planning "a $1.8 billion mixed-use development with 1,000 condominium-hotel units, 600 residential condos, a 600-room hotel, an 80,000-square-foot casino and 200,000 square feet of retail space." As often happens in the media, the newspaper did not interview Gary. In fact, these gargantuan plans were what Centex, his partner, was considering for the Westward Ho site. This project would have constituted a massive roll of the proverbial dice, which was far from Gary's style.

Before he had to decide about any involvement in Centex's dream plan, Centex sold its majority shares in the property to Gary for $80 million in June 2006. In retrospect, Gary believes Centex foresaw that the housing bubble was about to burst. "[T]he worldwide rise in house prices," reported The Economist at the time, "is the biggest bubble in history."

However, Gary wasn't overly worried about the housing bubble. He is not a man to fear the future and was happy to buy Centex's interest in the casino. As it turned out, the housing bubble was something to fear, and Las Vegas was one of the hardest-hit areas in the nation.

Fortunately, only three months after Gary acquired the Centex interest, a longtime casino owner intervened. In July 2006, Gary was driving from his home in Henderson, Nevada, which is about 15 miles southeast of downtown Las Vegas, to his office on East Warm Springs Road, which is a mile south of McCarran International Airport. As usual, the sun was shining and, as usual, the temperature was heading north of 100 degrees F. And, as usual, Gary's outfit was a polo shirt and shorts. His cell phone rang. Chuck Atwood, the vice chairman and former CFO of Harrah's Entertainment, was on the line. Harrah's Entertainment was one of the world's largest casino operators with, at the time, 48 properties in 13 states and five countries outside the U.S. Atwood asked if Gary could meet him within the hour at Atwood's office at Harrah's Casino on the Strip. Gary agreed and went directly to Harrah's, still in shorts and a polo shirt.

Half an hour later, Gary was sitting in Atwood's office, where he met Jonathan Halkyard, Harrah's CFO and a senior vice president, and John Knott, Harrah's real estate broker. They tendered an offer to buy the Westward Ho casino from Gary. At first, he couldn't figure out why they wanted it. The demolition permit was issued in January 2006 and the buildings were slated for implosion, which eventually took place in March 2007.

Per the map opposite, the Westward Ho site was located beside the 63-acre site of the famous Stardust Resort and Casino, which was still open. The Stardust closed in November 2006 and was demolished four months later.

Gary would later find out that Harrah's planned to orchestrate a land swap with Boyd Gaming: the 18-acre Westward Ho site for the 1.8-acre Barbary Coast, which Boyd owned. Harrah's wanted the Barbary since it was situated in the middle of several properties (including the Flamingo Hotel and Casino, Imperial Palace, and Harrah's Las Vegas Hotel and Casino) that it owned at one of the world's busiest intersections. It was the prime location on the Vegas Strip: the nexus of Las Vegas Boulevard and Flamingo Road. Harrah's had acquired Caesars Palace across the street in 2005. Securing the Barbary would enable Harrah's to create a coherent plan for three-quarters of the center of the Vegas Strip.

Boyd, on the other hand, owned the Stardust and, Atwood knew, would very much want the contiguous Westward Ho site. This would enable Boyd to create a master plan for the 87 total acres it would then hold at the north end of the Strip. Atwood was already in talks for the land swap with Elis Landau, the CFO of Boyd Gaming.

After only an hour of negotiation, Gary walked out of Harrah's as the biggest winner in the casino's history. He had made an agreement to sell the hotel and casino for $280 million, and the deal closed in September 2006. After paying the real estate commission and Centex's equity, plus $10 million to demolish the Westward Ho, Gary cleared $108 million—without having to invest a penny in renovating the Westward Ho or having to change out of his shorts and polo and into one of his few business suits.

"That was the best deal I've ever made," Gary said with a broad smile.

Actually, the best part of the deal was yet to come. After Harrah's and Boyd swapped casinos, Boyd embarked on planning and building Echelon Place, a $4 billion mega-resort and casino. In this case, however, the big house—the U.S. economy—won. The Great Recession descended and Las Vegas was pummeled. Construction of Echelon Place was halted in August 2008 after only a few floors had been erected. Boyd eventually sold the site to the Genting Group for a loss of $994 million.

As a result of the casino swap and then the Great Recession, both Harrah's (which became Caesars) and Boyd struggled financially for years. In fact, Caesars Entertainment and Caesars Entertainment Operating Company were forced to declare bankruptcy in January 2015.

The Westward Ho Hotel and Casino opened in 1963. It was shuttered in November 2005 and then demolished in 2006.

Today, Resorts World Las Vegas, a Chinese-themed casino and resort, is under construction on the Echelon site. This mega-project is scheduled to open in 2020 for a total cost of about $7.2 billion.

Gary dodged one large caliber recession bullet, but he wouldn't survive the economic downturn unscathed.

During this same period in 2006, a much larger deal than the Westward Ho was brewing for Gary. He was approached by Goldman Sachs' real estate investment wing, Archon Hospitality LP, to buy 143 hotels. After negotiations, Archon bought 140 hotels in two tranches (130 and then 10) for $1.309 billion. After paying off his debts on the hotels, Gary had more than $735 million in cash.

Fyke remembered the deal well. Not only was it Gary's biggest score, the deal changed her career path—for a while. She decided to leave Gary's employ

Gary Tharaldson, who typically wears a polo shirt to work, reviews plans for a new hotel in Las Vegas with Jeff McKay (left), a project manager at Dakota Legacy Group, a company co-owned by Gary and Rick Larson (right) in Fargo.

---

with the hotels to ensure proper asset management. This was also her time, she believed, to go out on her own.

She soon found out, however, that working for Gary was the best option by far. The entire hospitality industry agreed. In 2010, Gary was awarded the first Hunter Investment Conference Inaugural Award for Excellence and Inspiration. The Hunter Conference is the premier hotel investment conference in the U.S., and 40 percent of attendees are hotel owners.

"I have known and greatly admired our honoree, Gary Tharaldson, for 20 years," said Daryl Nickel, the Executive Vice President for Corporate Development for the Marriott Corporation, who gave the award presentation speech. "Like so many of you and thousands in our industry, I am a beneficiary of Gary's prolific development and design, construction and operational innovations and his leadership, generosity and inspiration to others."

Two years later, in 2012, Fyke was back with Gary running his hotels in the third incarnation of his hospitality empire. Fyke was enjoying family life with her husband and four children without a serious worry. Before she could recover from the shock of Gary telling her he might have to declare bankruptcy, he said, "I want you to know that you, your family and our employees are going to be OK."

Fyke felt both relief and a deep concern for Gary. It was so typical of him, she thought, to be worried first about others. Gary had devoted hundreds of millions of dollars through the years to benefit family members, friends and employees, including Fyke's family, whom he had made into millionaires.

Also in 1999, Gary established an Employee Stock Ownership Plan and Trust (ESOP) to benefit all of his employees. He sold 214 of his hotels to the ESOP for no money down. He also served as the ESOP's trustee until 2006 to make sure that the hotels would continue to be run well. In 2014, these hotels were sold, precipitating a payout in 2016 of more than $500 million to the remaining 4,000 participants across the country. Over $100 million had already been paid out to former employees as they left. This $600 million was money Gary could have kept. And if he had kept the money, he would have used it to build more hotels and make an additional $600 million. Today, he would be a richer but not a happier man.

After cashing out in 2006, Gary invested most of the $735 million in extensive land holdings; and he also built an ethanol plant for a projected $225 million in Casselton, North Dakota, about 40 miles east of Fargo. There were costly delays due to technological and equipment issues, and the plant ended up costing $300 million.

After the Great Recession hit, Gary began to have cash flow problems. His land assets were not liquid, nor were they generating a profit. In fact, these holdings were costing significant amounts of money in maintenance and taxes. At the same time, he still owned 21 hotels, had four scheduled to open later that year and had 29 hotels in the construction pipeline, which meant they were supposed to open in 2009 or 2010. He put a hold on the 29 hotels since he couldn't afford to finance their construction. Yet his open hotels were not numerous enough to render sufficient profits to cover his overall debt service and building and operation costs.

Gary sold four hotels for much less than their value before the recession; he needed the cash to keep going. Even so, Gary was in serious trouble and his legacy was threatened. He certainly didn't want to sell all his hotels at painful discounts. Would his business ventures survive? Gary had never declared bankruptcy before and he hated the idea, although many of America's most successful companies and individuals have taken advantage of bankruptcy laws to protect personal assets, and to restructure their businesses and reemerge.

Gary's lawyers were adamant: He must declare bankruptcy.

"If I have to file," Gary responded, "I still want to pay every one of my banks back the full amount that they are owed."

Gary was advised strongly by lawyers not to do so, to simply get out of this situation and not pay anybody back. But then "the banks get screwed," Gary said, "and I've always been treated well by my banks."

This was honorable, to be sure, but would also make rebuilding his businesses more difficult and certainly more time consuming, if even possible. Approaching 67 years of age, Gary was running out of time as well as cash. Would he lose it all and go back to zero where he started? Or would Gary find a way to recover and keep adding zeros to his net worth?

———————————

To comprehend Gary's crisis—and to understand the lessons his successes and failures demonstrate—it is necessary, as well as intensely interesting, to recount the story of where Gary came from and how he became so wealthy in the first place.

It's also highly instructive to see how someone born without privilege or material advantage overcame barriers that prevent most people from succeeding, including those born with means. Opportunity is a road open to all, but there is no easy GPS app to get there.

This story illuminates how commerce and its entrepreneurs, who power the entire American economic enterprise, work. As Frank Borman, the astronaut who served as commander of Apollo 8, the first U.S. mission to fly around the moon, put it: "Capitalism without bankruptcy is like Christianity without Hell."

Only against this background can Gary's ultimate triumphs and current renaissance be fully appreciated.

Beginnings:
Family & Career

1866-1981

CHAPTER ONE

Dazey & Homesteading on the Prairie

In 1862, Abraham Lincoln
signed the Homestead Act,
a bill opening one half million
square miles of territory in
the western United States
for settlement.

Peter Agre

GARY DEAN THARALDSON was born in Dazey, North Dakota, on October 17, 1945, the second of six children. Located in a farming area in east central North Dakota, Dazey is, as Garrison Keillor would say, "not the end of the world, but you can see it from there."

Dazey was founded in 1883 on land donated by Charles Turner Dazey, who ran a "bonanza farm" in the Red River Valley. Bonanza farms were large farms established in the American West to take advantage of new technologies, such as the steam engine. Cheap land and cheap labor enabled the formation of 10,000- to 100,000-acre farms, mostly wheat, that operated more like factories than family farms. The first bonanza farms were established in the Red River Valley in the 1870s.

The city of Dazey sits on the western edge of the Red River Valley about 90 miles northwest of Fargo. The area is literally flat as a pancake with rich black alluvial loam soil that supports a varied and highly productive agricultural economy. Dazey's population peaked in 1920 at 293 people and then declined slowly but relentlessly for the next eight decades, as did the entire state. But the advances in fracking and hydraulic drilling—the new, revolutionary petroleum and natural gas extraction technologies—that precipitated the oil boom of the 2000s in the Bakken oil fields of western North Dakota have acted as a population transfusion, attracting tens of thousands of people to the state. In the decade 2000-2010, North Dakota's population increased by 5 percent to 672,591. In 2000, Dazey had 91 residents, which grew by 14 percent to 104 over the next decade. Today, the US Census Bureau estimates that Dazey has a population of 102.

Gary grew up there in the 1940s and 50s, and in 1960, Dazey's population stood at 226. His generation tended to leave town for higher education and jobs. Families who remained behind are certainly not wealthy today. The median value of a house is $50k and the median household income is $36k, which is only two-thirds of the national and 60 percent of the state household medians.

Charles Turner Dazey, the town's founder, left Dazey soon after it was established. He returned to Illinois to seek success, which he found by writing Broadway plays and then movie scripts for Hollywood films in the silent era, including "Shifting Sands," starring screen legend Gloria Swanson. There was no movie theater in Dazey when "Shifting Sands" was released in 1918, and no such venue has been built since then. The town's only artwork consists of a new metallic welcome sign, pictured on the opposite page. It is nearly big enough to conceal the entire town.

Dazey has no street signs and although street names appear on town maps, residents don't use them. As when Gary was growing up, so-and-so's house was described as two streets down and one over. None of Dazey's streets have asphalt paving. There is a post office in the same small building as the American Legion. The only functioning business is Punky's Bar & Grill at the east end of Dazey's main street. Across the street from Punky's is a sign on the lawn of a house reading "Convenience Store." No hours of convenience are posted.

There is a rundown Lutheran church, where Gary's family attended Sunday services. About five miles east of Dazey on a dirt road sits a small Roman Catholic church surrounded by open fields.

A block west of Punky's at the corner of East Street is Dazey's community center, a one-story corrugated steel structure. Another block west is the Assembly of God church, the only recently built (meaning post-1950) structure. It's a simple concrete block building covered with white tin siding.

During Dazey's heyday (perhaps "hay-day" was more accurate), several brick structures stood on the current sites of the community center and the Assembly of God church, and on the now empty lots in between these buildings and across the street. A long-gone railway depot was established in the 1880s, followed by various businesses, including lumber, grocery and general merchandise stores, blacksmith shops, banks, meat markets, restaurants and hotels, drugstores and a confectionary shop. A telephone company and the Farmers Co-operative Elevator were established in the early 1900s, along with the town newspaper, the Dazey Herald. After two damaging fires in the town, the Dazey Fire Department was founded in 1912.

In the 1890s, Gary's great-grandfather, Daniel Tharaldson, worked as a carpenter building the Larson Mercantile Building, a three-story, wood-framed structure with a 50-foot storefront known as "the Big Store," which over the decades housed various stores on the main floor and a community

Gary standing in front of the new community sign at the entrance to Dazey, ND, where he grew up.

---

hall on the second floor. In 1903, the third floor was removed and brick veneer was added to the exterior. The Dazey Grocery was the last business to occupy the Big Store, which was shuttered in 1979 and later torn down.

In November 1980, Gary's paternal grandmother, Emma Tharaldson, wrote a short autobiography that chronicles family history and offers insight into the family traits, such as perseverance and self-sufficiency.

Emma began the account, writing: "I have had a very good, long life and enjoyed it all. There has been plenty of work to do but I was young and it didn't hurt me at all as I still have good health at 86 years of age." The work is dedicated to her nine children, 36 grandchildren and 35 great-grandchildren.

We learn that in 1873, at age 33, Daniel Tharaldson, Gary's great-grand-father (and Emma's future father-in-law), left the family farm in Fosnes, Norway, and immigrated to the U.S. He then made his way to Eau Claire, Wisconsin, which was a common destination for Norwegians. Almost a third of Norway's population, numbering about 750,000 people, immigrated to Canada and the U.S. between 1835 and 1900. Most of these immigrants settled in Minnesota, Wisconsin, Montana and the Dakotas, as well as in Manitoba, Saskatchewan and Alberta.

Daniel worked as a carpenter and painter in the Eau Claire area. In 1880, he married Ingnora Oveson, 29, who was also born in Norway, and a year later, he became an American citizen. In the spring of 1882, Daniel and Ingnora journeyed to the Fargo Land Office to file for a quarter-section (160 acres) homestead in Lake Town township, about six miles northwest of Dazey.

The pioneer couple first settled on their claim on June 2, 1882. "It is told that it snowed that first night," Emma recounted. "Daniel commenced building a 16′ x 16′ frame house and five acres of sod was broken that first summer." The first crop, harvested in the fall of 1883, consisted of 60 bushels of wheat. By 1888, half the homestead's sod was broken for crops. A year later, testimony of proof of homestead was rendered in the county courthouse in Valley City.

The Homestead Act allowed settlers to get 160 acres of free land by living on and improving the land for five years. Or, after two years, the homesteader could buy the land for $1.25 an acre. The first wave of settlers to North Dakota arrived in the 1870s and 80s. Under the Timber Culture Act (1873), a homesteader could claim an additional 160 acres by raising crops or planting 10 acres of trees. Also, the Pre-emption Act (1841) allowed a settler to buy 160 acres of unsettled government land for $1.25 an acre. The Northern Pacific Railroad was given about 25 percent of North Dakota's land mass, which was sold for $3 to $5 per acre.

The headstone in Dazey's Lutheran cemetery for Johanna Olson, Gary's great-great-grandmother on his father's side, who died in 1892.

Daniel's mother, Johanna Olson, also immigrated to America and, in 1886, filed for a 160-acre homestead adjoining her son's farm to the east, as shown on the following page. Johanna died in 1892, after which Daniel broke sod on and cultivated both his and his mother's homesteads. As Emma wrote, Daniel and Ingnora "realized the immigrant's dream of being a landowner and prospered under rather harsh conditions." The couple had three children, including Emil (Gary's grandfather, born in 1886) and two daughters, Lula (born in 1887) and Ida (born in 1891).

In 1902, however, Ingnora died of consumption (tuberculosis) at the age of 51. A year later, Daniel suffered a fatal heart attack. This left their son, Emil, just 17 years of age, to take care of his younger sisters. Their landholdings are shown on the 1910 plat map on the following page.

In total, Emil was farming almost a full section, which included the original homestead, his grandmother's quarter and a third quarter, which he

LAKE TOWN TOWNSHIP – 1910
Barnes County, North Dakota

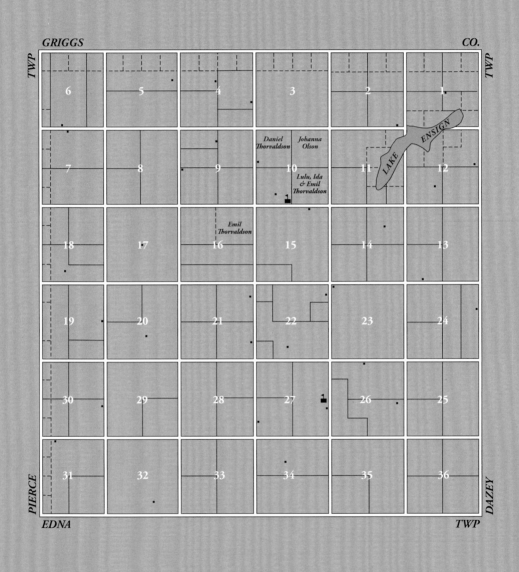

The plat map for Barnes County, ND, in 1910.

Emma (nee Christenson) and Emil Tharaldson,
Gary's grandparents on his father's side.

purchased. Emil had also acquired a quarter section diagonally across the road to the southwest. This quarter included a few acres set aside for the local elementary school—where, coincidentally, Emma would teach before they married.

At five years of age, Emma's father, Hans Christenson, emigrated with his mother and grandmother from Sel, Norway, in 1870. That same year they filed for a quarter-section homestead near Butterfield, Minnesota. Hans' mother died soon afterwards and his father is never mentioned in Emma's account, indicating that he had died earlier in Norway or had immigrated earlier and passed away before his family arrived. Hans was raised by an aunt and then adopted by another aunt and uncle.

In 1866, Emma's maternal grandparents emigrated from the same region of Norway as her father's family. "They had been seven weeks in a ship coming across the Atlantic and had a harrowing time of it," wrote Emma.

"I remember hearing that at one time a sea serpent laid itself across the bow of the boat and caused some alarm for the passengers. In the morning, it was found that the serpent had removed itself from the boat. From New York, they traveled by ox cart to southern Minnesota."

Emma's maternal grandfather also filed for a quarter-section homestead near Butterfield, Minnesota. Emma's mother "was born in a covered wagon on October 19, 1871, just as the family had gotten to their homestead. Her father had … prepared a dugout home with a thatched roof."

More harrowing than sea serpents was withstanding harsh weather in such primitive conditions. "During the winter months of those early years, Grandpa Joe walked to Worthington, many miles to the west, every Sunday night to work during the week. Here he helped to build the first railroad across Southern Minnesota," Emma recounted. "Once following a three-day blizzard, Grandpa was anxious to return home to check on his family. Reaching the site where he thought his home was located, he was startled to find only a mass of whiteness. … The family pet, upon hearing the sound of Grandpa's shoes walking on the cold, crisp snow, began to bark. Grandpa hurriedly dug the snow away to rescue his family."

After Emma's parents married in 1892, they moved 185 miles northeast to a farm they purchased near Fish Lake, Minnesota. Emma was born there in 1894, and seven years later, the family moved to a farm near Wylie, Minnesota, about 35 miles east of Grand Forks, North Dakota. In 1905, they moved to a farm north of Leal, North Dakota, and then two years later they rented a larger farm near Dazey, shown on the plat map as section 23.

Emma attended the local Lake Town public school and then Dazey's school from the 5th grade through high school. She graduated in 1915 and then attended Valley City Normal School to become a teacher. In the fall, Emma began teaching at a rural school in Edna, about 15 miles southeast of Dazey. For the next five years, Emma taught elementary school in the area, including at the school in plat map. Her last assignment was at the Sibley Trail public school, the next town due east of Dazey, where she was paid $75 per month.

GARY THARALDSON FAMILY TREE

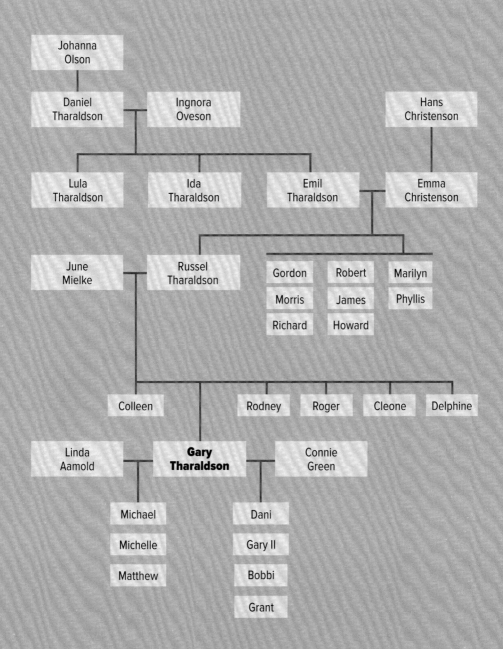

At 4 a.m. on Thursday, May 25, 1916, Emil was alone on his farm taking refuge in the wood-framed house, which he had recently built, as a huge storm rolled across the open prairie. Another smaller storm had passed through earlier and then the winds rose again, this time stronger and armed not only with sheets of rain but also hail.

"Barns and houses were blown over and other damage was done," reported the Dazey Herald. "Emil Tharaldson's new house west of town was completely destroyed and Emil was quietly (sic) badly hurt. He was in the house … and carried with the building when it left its foundation. He was thrown first from one side of the building to the other as it was carried in the air and landed among debris when the house was finally dropped to the ground." Emil was found by a neighbor, who pulled him from the wreckage. However, most of the house was never found, and it soon became local lore that the missing parts of the structure were dropped into Lake Ensign, a small, enclosed, swampy body of water, shown in the upper right corner of the plat map on page 24.

The next year, Emil signed up for a storm of a different kind, World War I, which rained blood instead of water. From April 1917 to April 1919, Emil served in the U.S. Army Medical Corps. After the war, General Karl von Einem, commander of Germany's 3rd Army, called American troops the "most honorable" and "bravest of our enemies." During the American occupation after the war, a German mayor testified that, "[The Americans] are wonderfully mild-mannered men and a great contrast to the domineering attitude of our own soldiers. Your troops, not even one, have spoken a single disagreeable word to anyone, and when we offered them wood for cooking and heating purposes they accepted with what seemed to be a certain shyness."

During his service, mostly in France, Emil sent Emma Christenson boxes of candy anonymously. "Soon after," Emma recounted, "his letters would arrive and I knew who the gifts were from."

Emma and Emil were married on January 1, 1920, and moved into a new house he built on their farm. A year later their firstborn, Howard, arrived and, in another 18 months, Russel, "a black-haired baby boy," was born. Seven more children joined the family, the youngest born in 1935.

June and Russel Tharaldson with their three eldest children—left to right, Gary, Rodney and Connie—in 1948.

When Russel was about six years old, he and Howard were seen "hard at work" by neighbors who "came into the house to tell me what the boys were doing. I went to them and they looked at them [the neighbors] and they looked at me and said, 'Two big boys fixing Dad's binder,'" Emma recalled. "By this time, they had broken a couple of wheels with cogs. Needless to say, their dad had more repairing to do."

"My husband always preferred to stay home with [the children] whenever I had to go somewhere," Emma wrote. "He was a very good cook so I didn't worry. He had learned from his mother and then from practical experience … He also learned bread baking. Emil taught me many ways to cook."

The 1928 plat map shows that the original homestead had been taken over by Emil's sister Lula and her husband, and it was registered in her married name. The other quarter sections remained in Emil's name. Fortunately, the Tharaldsons survived the dry years of the 1920s, when Emma's parents lost their farm. But then they lost almost everything during the Great Depression in the 1930s. The next available plat map, published in 1952, shows that Emma owned the quarter section next to the quarter Emil had purchased, which included school property. But the four quarters, owned by Emil on the 1910 map, were no longer in the family's possession.

Emil died suddenly in 1954 at 66 years of age. Gary remembers his grandfather as quiet and reserved, or perhaps he was simply tired after raising two younger sisters, nine children and, at the same time, working a full section of demanding farmland. His son, Howard, lived at home and farmed the remaining quarter section into the 1950s, when Emma moved into a small house in Dazey.

By 1968, the last quarter of farmland owned by a Tharaldson had been sold, ending the family's pioneering version of the American dream.

Gary in the farmyard on the family's original homestead,
about four miles northwest of Dazey, ND.

CHAPTER TWO

Early Years in Obscurity, North Dakota

When I look back, I'm glad I grew
up in small town. There, it's just you,
your family and whatever
you make of it.

Champ Bailey

GARY'S MOTHER, June Grace Mielke, grew up on a farm near Marion, North Dakota, a small town about 30 miles south of Dazey. Her family moved to Dazey when June was in high school. She met Russel in her senior year when she worked part time—perhaps presciently—in the restaurant of the town's only small hotel, owned by her older brother. She graduated secondary school in June 1942 and married Russel that fall in Moorhead, Minnesota. June was 18 years of age and Russel was 20.

June and Russel's first child, Colleen (known as "Connie"), arrived in July 1944. Fifteen months later, on October 17, 1945, Gary was born the second child, just like his father. Rodney arrived in February 1947 and Roger was born in September 1949. The last two children were girls: Cleone in September 1954 and Delphine in April 1959.

The first floor of the Tharaldsons' wood-framed house was only 676 square feet. The second floor was even smaller since the roof slanted acutely on all four sides. The house, at the corner of 2nd and Corbett Streets, had neither running water nor indoor plumbing while Gary was growing up. The family drew water from a pump beside a house across the street. Since there was no tub or shower, Gary recalls washing up in a large basin. The household did have a radio and record player, and Gary remembers the TV set that joined the family in the mid-1950s.

Russel worked as a carpenter and struggled to support his family. Gary recalls that his father was well respected in his trade. He showed up early, worked late and was both very efficient and skilled. Still, wages were low, and today the family would be considered as living below the poverty line. Fortunately, there were no affluent families in town for comparison.

"I was just a kid growing up and never really thought about being poor," Gary said. "I loved sports and I never felt sorry for myself or my family."

When Gary was in the 6th grade, his father was finally able to buy a car. Before then, Russel walked to work and had to arrange for a neighbor to drive his wife to the hospital when she went into labor. For shopping needs beyond basics, the family took a train, "really just like a passenger car that came through and went all the way to Valley City. We would buy stuff and catch the train back home."

In his junior year, Gary is the shortest member of the North Central High School's varsity basketball team, the Corvairs (20-4 and district title).

Beside the house was a large garden where June grew much of the fresh fruits and vegetables she preserved for her growing brood. A barn behind the house on the half-acre lot housed several dairy cows. Russel sold cream to a local creamery and, like many rural families of that time, the family drank the unpasteurized milk. [Today, the Center for Disease Control and Prevention says that the risk of becoming ill from consuming raw milk is nine times greater than from drinking pasteurized milk, but the risk of serious illness is very small, and raw milk has nutritional benefits.]

On Sundays, the Tharaldson family walked a few blocks to Our Savior's Lutheran Church for services and Sunday school. Gary recalled the yearly Christmas play as "special" because he and his siblings were involved.

Now when he watches his children playing sports or participating in school events, he remembers his own childhood. It's remarkable how different their lives are to his—and how similar. Each generation had loving parents who imparted a Christian moral code, kindness, discipline, optimism, a competitive spirit and a strong work ethic.

Gary still attends church on Sunday, although he never mentions it. His wife, Connie, also goes to weekly Bible class and Gary sometimes joins her. Christianity for Gary comes down to "being good to everyone. What I learned as a child at church was to treat everybody really well."

From kindergarten through 8th grade, Gary attended Dazey Public School, with about 10 students per class and one class per grade. What Gary remembers is not so much grammar, history or geography, but basketball and other sports.

Although baseball was always Gary's favorite, he played every sport the school offered.

In the 6th grade, Gary played on the school's basketball team with the 7th- and 8th-graders, even though he was the shortest teammate by far. By the 10th grade, he stood no more than 5'2".

Gary's senior photo from North Central High School, fall 1963.

"I made the basketball team because I could shoot," Gary recounted. "My brother Rodney and I used to go out in the snow banks in the winter and shoot basketballs all the time on our outside basketball court with our jackets on."

"Oh, that Gary, he could sure make baskets," his mother said after a game in which his team beat a much better squad. His mother's praise pleased him immensely.

"I had a really good game and scored about 12 points, which was a lot in those days."

In 1959, Gary started secondary school at North Central High School in Rogers, North Dakota, about 10 miles south of Dazey. His grades were half Bs and half Cs, which reflected his lack of interest in studies or, more accurately, his love of sports. Academics could never compete for Gary's attention the way a bouncing ball or Louisville Slugger could.

At North Central, he played guard on the varsity basketball team for all four years and also played second base on the baseball team. In his senior year, North Central fielded a football team for the first time and Gary played halfback. They finished in second place in the local conference. "Not bad for a first-year team," Gary recalled with justifiable pride.

"In sports, I was a quiet leader," Gary said. "I led more by example than I did by being the rah-rah type of guy. Even after graduating from college, getting up and speaking was not what I liked to do."

This quiet leader was also the classic little guy always competing with much bigger classmates to make the varsity team and then taking on taller and often more talented opponents in conference games. And winning. Not always, of course, but often enough to learn how to overcome limitations and achieve goals. One of the important life lessons he learned was that winning—or more precisely, putting maximum effort into winning regardless of outcome—is far better than complaining. The notion that he was a victim of poverty or heredity or any other circumstance was not going to define Gary Tharaldson.

As well as constructing buildings, Gary's father often tore down old structures for Richard Grotberg, a farmer in Wimbledon, a small town about 20 miles west of Dazey. Grotberg ran a demolition business on the side and there was no shortage of aging and abandoned buildings throughout the state. On weekends and summers after his freshman year in high school, Gary worked alongside his father. Grotberg took a liking to Gary and asked if the teen could come live with him and his parents. The farmer wanted help with daily chores, and he could see how difficult it was for Gary's father to feed and care for a growing family of six children, then ages 6 through 15. Nor was there much room for Gary in the house.

Gary lived with the Grotbergs through his sophomore year and the following summer. He worked after school and on weekends as a farmhand for room and board and $50 per month—not a lot of money, but more than Gary had ever had before. With his pay, he could buy his own clothes and

In Dazey, Gary talks with Phil Quick, a first cousin and son of his father's sister Phyllis, outside Phil's house. Phil worked as a mail carrier throughout his career. At the end of the street to the right is the house where their grandmother, Emma Tharaldson, lived in her final years—decades, actually. Emma passed away in 1987 at 93 years of age. Gary recalls her tending lush flower beds and a large garden, all of which is overgrown now.

sports equipment. Happily, Gary was still allowed time to play on sports teams at school, which meant his chores sometimes had to be done in the late evening.

Remarkably, this living arrangement proved to be Gary's initiation into entrepreneurial thinking. Grotberg loved telling Gary about the profit he made contracting to demolish old buildings, showing the high schooler his costs and total revenue.

"I was amazed at how much he made so quickly," Gary recalled.

Grotberg was also very ambitious. He told Gary he was going to buy lots of land with his earnings and become "a really big farmer"—which eventually he did.

Gary Tharaldson talks with childhood friend, Gary Hare, on Dazey's main street in front of the only remaining establishment in the town, Punky's Bar & Grill. Gary Hare, who is four years younger than Gary, recalls how Gary and his cousin Jerry taught him to play basketball. Gary Hare does maintenance and landscaping work in Dazey and was also the town mayor.

Not only did Grotberg profit from ripping down old buildings, but he made additional money selling the lumber from the job.

"It was a nasty business because all those old buildings were so dirty," Gary recalled with a laugh. "But he was such a fired-up individual. It was fun listening to him talk about all the big things he was going to do in the future. At home, my dad was not an entrepreneur, so I didn't have anybody to spur me on."

Not surprisingly, Gary caught Grotberg's entrepreneurial spirit. In Gary's senior year, a farmer named Steele saw Gary and his brother Rodney and their cousin Jerry tearing down a school for Grotberg near Pingree, about 20 miles north of Jamestown. Steele asked the boys if they could tear down an old building on his property. After going with him to see the structure, Gary gave him a bid: $400.

"We took time off from the school project, which we were working on on an hourly basis, and went over and did the farmer's building," Gary recounted. "We tore it down so quickly the farmer asked for a discount, so we took $300 and still made $100 each, which was big money then."

This event lit a fire in Gary's spirit. He decided to become a business owner rather than work for hourly wages as his father did.

Gary returned to live at home during 11th grade. He was glad to be back with his family but with college looming, saving money was necessary.

During the summer before senior year, Gary lived at Doug Quick's farm near Dazey and worked as a farm hand. Like Grotberg, Quick had an entrepreneurial spirit. He took Gary with him on trips to deliver hay bales to Portland, 75 miles northeast of Dazey. In the truck as they drove, Quick talked often about acquiring more land and building a much bigger farm—which eventually he did.

Then Gary spent his senior year living and working on Doug's brother Gary's dairy farm, which was five miles south of Doug's farm. Again, Gary was allowed to play on his high school sports teams and finished his chores late into the evening and on weekends. He also had to wake up at 5 a.m. every morning to milk cows. However, Gary Quick insisted on driving him to school in Rogers every morning. It was a kindly act but also one of the scariest experiences in Gary Tharaldson's life.

"He was a crazy driver who drove 70 miles per hour no matter the weather," Gary recalled. "I held onto my seat the whole way every day."

Gary was treated well by both Quick brothers, as by Grotberg. This ethos of taking good care of employees was impressed upon Gary and stayed with him as an employer. Throughout his career, Gary would endeavor to inspire his workers to perform at the highest level and to reward them for their efforts.

It would be easy to say that Gary came from nothing, although that was close to the truth in material terms. But his parents, as well as his grandparents, were very loving and taught him life's most essential lessons. While his grandfather Emil was quiet and distant by the time Gary grew up, Emil had raised his siblings and his children with kindness and patience, which was an invaluable family heirloom.

Emma and Emil's nine children provided Gary and his siblings with 29 first cousins, along with dozens of second cousins. Most of these families eventually moved to the Minneapolis-St. Paul area, but they usually returned to Dazey for Thanksgiving, which was celebrated at Emil and Emma's house on the farm. Even after Emma moved into Dazey, the family congregated at her much smaller house there.

Gary recalls happy gatherings filled with laughter—adults talking, kids playing and multi-generational games of canasta, one of the most popular card games of the 1950s. Gary and cousin Jerry often visited grandmother Emma at other times to play canasta, which she loved doing.

Although the Tharaldsons were thoroughly Norwegian, Gary doesn't recall any particular Norwegian customs the family had retained from Norway—other than several Norwegian dishes involving dumplings and blood sausage. Gary's mother's family was German in origin, and she had six brothers and two sisters. But the family migrated to Oregon early in Gary's life, so the influence of his German heritage was far less pronounced.

Norway was one of the least populous European nations, yet so many Norwegians emigrated here that by 1900 they comprised a quarter of North Dakota's population. A Northern Great Plains tale held that one could walk all the way from Garrison Dam, which is 68 miles mostly north and a bit west of Bismarck to the state's northwest corner, where the Red River flows into Manitoba—a journey of about 300 miles—on land solely owned by ethnic Norwegians.

"The Norwegians' ethnic identity is a curious combination of pride and humility," wrote John M. Pederson, PhD, Professor of History, Economics and Social Science at Mayville (North Dakota) State University. As the reader will see throughout this book, this paradox of pride and humility reflects in Gary's personality. Rightly proud of his accomplishments and the companies he has built, Gary exhibits remarkable humility and gratitude for the efforts of his employees, friends and family on his behalf.

Also intrinsic to the Norwegian character is a strong work ethic, which Gary inherited—along with the human capital only a solid family and a good upbringing can bestow. Of course, no family is perfect, but for the Tharaldsons there was more than enough warmth, morality, faith and love to equip Gary for success.

As readers will see, Gary could also be too trusting of associates and employees, which sometimes cost him dearly. Perhaps it was his Midwest upbringing in a small town populated with working-class families who prized sincerity and truthfulness that rendered Gary vulnerable.

Many people grow up in struggling circumstances without achieving financial greatness. But rags-to-riches stories are an integral part of American mythology, both as fascinating narratives and blueprints for success. Harold Hamm, for example, was born the same year as Gary as the youngest of 13 children of Oklahoma sharecroppers and is now worth $14.5 billion. Hamm serves as the chairman and CEO of Continental Resources, an oil and natural gas exploration and production company with large holdings in the Bakken, among other major oil and gas plays.

Both men shared an inexhaustible supply of ambition and determination. Gary learned about the value of ambition from the farmers he worked with as a teen. He recalled shivering in the pre-dawn gloom on the way to the dairy barn as prairie winds drove the snow in horizontal brigades and the air temperature sank to -20 degrees F—or lower; he decided his career would not be farming, especially dairy farming. Since agriculture dominated the state's economy, this decision closed many career doors. What doors instead might open?

Following in his father's footsteps was another closed door—cemented shut in Gary's mind. After graduating from high school, he worked on a construction project with his father.

"He could do any task better than the other workers," Gary recalled.

As a novice, Gary was paid $1.25 per hour, while his highly competent, experienced father made only $1.75 per hour.

Even as a child, Gary wanted to "do something big" in his life. Heading off to college the next fall, he still felt the same way. One of comedian George Carlin's favorite lines in his monologues was, "When I was young, I wanted to be somebody ... I should have been more specific." Wanting to be "something (completely unspecified) big" would easily fall into Carlin's jest. Typically, children want to do big things, and just as typically, this fades with time. Dreams shrink into what is seen as achievable and ambition becomes more specific—with lowered sights.

But Gary had no intention of lowering his aim, even if he wasn't sure what to aim at yet.

CHAPTER THREE

Business Basics
& Fear of Failure

Too many people are thinking
of security instead of opportunity.
They seem more afraid of life
than death.

James F. Byrnes

The business of America
is business.

Calvin Coolidge

FROM AUGUST 1963 TO MAY 1967, Gary attended Valley City State College in Valley City, 60 miles due west of Fargo. Valley City had 7,800 residents in the mid-1960s and the population has decreased 15 percent since then. The Sheyenne River runs northeast to southwest through Valley City, which is known as the "city of bridges" since there are nine bridges within the city limits and three more crossings on the outskirts. The Hi-Line Bridge was completed in 1908 and achieved fame as the longest bridge for its height—at 3,860 feet in length and 162 feet above the river—in the world at the time. The bridge was important in the war effort during World War I and II as a major link in the nation's coast-to-coast transportation system. Today, the Hi-Line Bridge bears freight trains, some with cars taking corn to, and ethanol from, Gary's ethanol plant in Casselton, about 38 miles east of Valley City.

At Valley City State College, Gary completed a bachelor's degree with a double major in business administration and physical education. It might be more accurate to say he majored in competition and minored in academics.

"You would not classify me as a good student," he admitted. "I didn't apply myself and ended up with 3.0 in business and phys ed, but only 2.0 in some other classes."

Since Gary's parents were unable to help him pay tuition or living expenses, he worked weekends to get by. Most of his free time and passion were devoted to playing intramural sports, including baseball and basketball. He also played on the varsity wrestling team's practice squad in his freshman year and on the varsity football team's practice squad in his junior year. The hard reality was that the varsity athletes "were better than I was."

Being realistic can also be liberating. As the proverbial notion puts it: When one door closes, another opens—even if, in this case, Gary had to build the entire structure in which the new door would hang. He would also enjoy playing amateur sports throughout his career, with a keen sense of his strengths and limitations.

On Gary's 21st birthday in 1966, while still a senior at Valley City State College, he married Linda Aamold, who was also a senior—but in high school. Linda was 18 years old in an era when marrying young was still common. The

This trailer was Gary and Linda's first home in Fargo. "I was so poor I couldn't take my wife out to eat," Gary said. The newlyweds lived here for four months during Gary's first year teaching in Leonard, ND. In Gary's second year, they moved to Leonard rather than commute.

couple met at a movie theater in Valley City through a mutual friend.

The following September, Gary began his professional life as a teacher at Leonard High School in Leonard, North Dakota, which is about 40 miles southwest of Fargo. The salary was $5,800, which was more than a third less than the average secondary school teacher wage nationwide, and a third less than state and national median family incomes. Gary never complained about his salary, however. Instead, he worked weekends doing various construction jobs, such as pouring concrete, to make extra money. At the same time, he started a master's in education degree program at North Dakota State University (NDSU) in Fargo.

"I always wanted to get ahead," Gary said about this period of teaching, studying and working construction. It was a simple statement that held much more force than mere aspiration.

With a new wife to support, who was also keen on business success, Gary started selling insurance in the summer after his first year of teaching. "But after about three weeks, I quit," Gary recounted, "because I just couldn't sell. I was still too shy and lacked confidence."

The insurance company's area manager quickly contacted Gary, listened to his reasons for quitting and offered to teach him how to sell. "I went out with him on calls, and after the first day, I said to myself, 'If that guy can do it, I can do it,'" Gary recalled. "What I needed was a change in attitude. The manager wasn't a good-looking guy and he was quite big, but he had a very positive attitude."

Gary succeeded at selling insurance for the rest of the summer and part-time during his second year of teaching. This was Gary's moment of trans-formation in business. "It was the difference that really changed me," he said. "After that I was fearless in business whenever there was risk of failure."

Gary and Linda Tharaldson with their three children—left to right, Matthew, Michael and Michelle—in 1982.

As actor Jack Lemmon put it, "Failure seldom stops you. What stops you is the fear of failure."

Teaching school also helped Gary mature. "I learned how to stand in front of a class and speak," he recalled. "When I started, I felt intimidated by the students and other staff members."

During his second year at Leonard High School, Gary began listening to motivational tapes, such as "Dare to Be Great" by Glenn W. Turner, who was the Tony Robbins of the late 1960s and 1970s. Turner was born into severe poverty to an unwed mother in South Carolina in 1934. He also was born with a cleft palate, which remained noticeable after surgical repair and left him with a lisp. Despite these obstacles, Turner became a charismatic speaker promoting a positive attitude to sales and other worthwhile endeavors. Turner built his cosmetics company's revenue up to $100 million in sales per year.

"I listened to his tapes over and over," Gary recounted. Turner was the quintessential little guy who overcame tremendous obstacles and succeeded through force of will, attitude and work ethic—the three things anyone can control.

"Turner's motto was, 'If you can conceive it and believe it, you can achieve it,'" Gary remembered as if he had just listened to the tape. Of course, he hadn't owned a tape deck for decades. Still, this motto was branded on Gary's consciousness and became the hallmark of his companies.

Gary took to heart the full range of Turner's dictums on the believe-achieve spectrum, such as: "Who is better at doing this than you? There should be no one better than you" and "You need to believe you're better than them at what you are doing because you can be."

"The motivational tapes really propelled me into believing that whatever I wanted to become in life, I could be the best," Gary said. "Who else could build 46 hotels in one year?" In his peak years in 1995 and 1996, Gary opened 46 and 44 hotels, respectively. Gary developed the capacity to set a sprinter's pace and keep it up for a marathon. Throughout the 1990s, as the reader will see, Gary built, opened and ran 30 new hotels per year on average.

Gary's salary, however, was never going to deliver him to the Turner-inspired Promised Land, even though he received an 8.6 percent raise to $6,300 for his second year of teaching. By the end of that school year, he had to take only one more course and complete his thesis to earn a master's degree. Then he would have had the option of taking an administrative position the next fall and earning another bump in salary.

But Gary took stock of his situation as summer approached. Would he spend July and August finishing his master's degree? One astonishing fact stuck out: He had earned as much selling insurance part time during the school year as he had teaching full time. Becoming a school principal or even a superintendent would not change that economic fact. Gary decided to leave education altogether in order to sell insurance full time.

Soon Gary's family responsibilities increased. Gary and Linda's first child, Michael, was born on March 2, 1969, followed by Michelle on March 10, 1971, and Matthew on April 11, 1978.

Throughout the 1970s, Gary learned five major lessons selling insurance that proved foundational for his future success in the hotel business:

First, Gary learned that starting one's own business is the best path to success.

In 1970, Gary moved his family to Bismarck where he became an area insurance sales manager, which involved hiring other agents who reported to him. He also secured a general agent's license from several insurance companies. The next year, Gary moved back to Valley City and, at only 26 years of age, went out on his own. He named the company the Tharaldson Insurance Agency, which became the first of a dozen companies he would found with his family name. Within three years, Gary had more than 100 agents working for him. Owning the company allowed Gary to make money not only from the policies and add-ons he sold but also from the products his agents sold.

Second, Gary learned the critical value of providing customers with the best product possible.

As a high school teacher, he began selling life and health insurance for the American Republic Insurance Company. The company provided leads with existing policyholders. "Insurance for hospital stays was on a per-day basis in those days," Gary explained, "so customers had to increase coverage for the

The Tharaldson Insurance team won the top division championship at the Sam McQuade Sr./Budweiser Charity Softball Tournament in 1983.

current cost of a hospital stay. The insurance company set it up so that you could go back and redo the same deals every few years."

Soon Gary determined that there were better insurance products with other companies. His company sold policies for Constitution Life, which was owned by Bankers Life and Casualty Company. "In many cases, I'd just go back to my American Republic clients, show them the difference between the two policies." This made it easy to sell the new policies.

"As in the hotel business, you want to sell the best products," Gary said. "If you don't, you're hurting the people, and it will come back and haunt you."

Armed with better insurance policies, Gary and his agents found it easy to sell to both existing and new clients. Serving the customer in the best way possible proved profitable and guaranteed repeat business. Customers remained loyal and rival companies had difficulty poaching Gary's clients.

Third, Gary learned the importance of timing and how to take advantage of opportunities.

In 1976, United Equitable started issuing nursing home insurance at the same time as the North Dakota Insurance Department required that every nursing home policy cover "what was called 'skilled' and intermediate care," Gary explained. "That broad coverage was much better for our clients."

Taking advantage of this scenario seems obvious in retrospect, but it's also true that most people miss obvious opportunities. "That's when I really started making money because we finally had a policy that was superior to anything else," Gary recounted and then added with a laugh: "Eventually the insurance companies got shellacked for these policies because they didn't anticipate how fast healthcare costs were going to increase."

Fourth, Gary learned that assets are the key to wealth creation.

When Gary was selling these policies, he developed a system. "Which people need nursing home insurance more than anybody else? People with assets," he recounted. "If I went into a city like Fargo, I couldn't determine who were ex-farmers. But in the rural areas, I would take a farmers' directory and then stop at a farm to ask if there was anyone 65 or older. If not, I would show the directory to the farmer who would usually identify farmers in the area at retirement age I could call on. Then the people who bought coverage would often give me the names of their friends."

Gary called on aging farmers because they most needed nursing home insurance, which they understood as asset protection insurance. They certainly did not want to lose the farm because of long-term nursing home costs. Importantly, Gary believed that the United Equitable product was the best on the market.

"It was such a great policy, I made six to eight sales a day, starting at 11 a.m. and finishing around 9 p.m.," Gary recalled. "I made up to $2000 a day and worked about three days a week. When I sold a $400 policy, my commission was $240. That was big money then."

Selling asset insurance also made Gary vividly aware of the value of assets. "I read a book back then saying there's only three ways to get rich. One way is to inherit it, and I wasn't going do that. The second method is by owning stock in a company. And the third way is through real estate. The bottom line is that you can't get rich through earned income since the government takes so much of your income."

Fifth, Gary learned how to build repeat business, which is crucial to making a profit and making the business sustainable.

Gary made an additional income every time a client renewed a nursing home policy, for example. "I received renewals on these sometimes for 25 years," he said. Repeat business is as critical in the hospitality business, as Gary would learn. If customers get the best product and service, they are very likely to come back and recommend the business or establishment to friends and relatives.

Now that Gary was making money, what was he going to do with it? It was still a very long way from insurance commissions to a billion-dollar empire. And there is no insurance policy in the world that can guarantee getting there. He already had an important insight that real estate was the key. But what kind of real estate?

The Gary Tharaldson
Express

1982-1999

CHAPTER FOUR

First Buildings & Hotels

Being good in business is the most
fascinating kind of art.
Making money is art and working is art
and good business is the best art.

Andy Warhol

Too much capitalism does
not mean too many capitalists,
but too few capitalists.

G.K. Chesterton

IN THE EARLY 1970s, a recession took hold of the economies of the U.S., Canada and Europe, ending the post-World War II economic boom. Unlike most previous recessions, this downturn was characterized by stagflation: high inflation, peaking at 9 percent, at the same time as unemployment remained high. The 1973 oil crisis, caused by the oil embargo by Arab states in retaliation for American support for Israel in the Yom Kippur War, was partly responsible. American Gross Domestic Product (GDP) fell from 5.6 percent in 1973 to -0.05 percent in 1974. From 1974 through 1981, unemployment averaged 7.2 percent while inflation averaged 9.3 percent—a deadly one-two punch for any economy.

Despite tough economic times, Gary's fortunes continued to improve. His yearly revenue jumped from less than $10,000 as an educator to $60,000 and then $70,000 in the mid-1970s. Gary's income continued to increase to $200,000 by the mid-1980s. One could say that sheer luck, a.k.a. Providence, played a significant role. Gary had the good fortune of selling insurance to people who needed the product and who had already made their money. There was also no competition at the time since other agencies in the area weren't targeting aging farmers to sell nursing home insurance.

Simultaneously, taxes were taking increasingly larger bites out of Gary's income. As a married head of household filing jointly, Gary paid a nominal rate of 50 percent on income over mid-$40,000s, and this rate rose steadily to 70 percent for income approaching $200,000.

As Gary contemplated his tax problem and the only open route he had to riches, he decided to dip his entrepreneurial toes into real estate by buying and "flipping" houses in the Valley City area, which he started to do in 1972. Just buying land, which had been the deep desire of his pioneering and farming forefathers, didn't solve his tax problem since "land is not a depreciable asset, but buildings are depreciable," he said. "I needed to own buildings, too."

At first, Gary renovated the properties himself and resold them, usually within six months to a year. High inflation rates guaranteed a substantial yield. If he held a property for more than six months, he had the additional advantage of paying long-term capital gains tax on profits, which was much lower than the nominal tax rate.

As the revenue Gary generated from his insurance business increased, he moved up to buying apartment buildings and hiring tradesmen to renovate and landscape the properties. He also contracted the renovators to build 20 single-family homes for a government-financed, low-income housing project, which were pre-sold. Gary's return on investment was certain and quick.

Gary's last major venture before entering the lodging industry involved buying the Straus Mall, a small indoor mall in downtown Valley City, in 1980. He oversaw limited renovations, installed several new clients and then sold the property after a year and a half. He didn't make any money but didn't lose any either.

"This was the wrong period for a mall," Gary said. "Interest rates were so high then, it was very difficult to make retail ventures work."

Malls would play a significant role in the future of Gary's hospitality business, but not as a mall owner.

———————————

In the late 1970s, Gary also bought a nine-unit apartment building in Valley City. "It was such a nice property, I collected rent for three or four years," Gary recalled. "But eventually I realized that having apartments with people calling all the time wasn't for me."

Gary began considering another kind of real estate: hotels. Guests check out after a day or two, so customer problems are short-lived. In 1982, Gary bought his first two hotels, a Super 8 in Valley City and another Super 8 in Devils Lake, about 120 miles north of Valley City. Hotels offered additional tax advantages to apartment buildings and houses. "There were investment tax credits then, too," he recalled. "So the furniture, fixtures and equipment I bought with the hotel and during that first year earned a 10 percent tax credit." Gary paid $500,000 for the Valley City hotel and $600,000 for the one in Devils Lake.

Gary Tharaldson's first hotel, a Super 8 he bought in 1982 as a tax shelter. The hotel is still operating under a different owner in Valley City, ND, and the hotel's exterior is finished in beige vinyl siding, in contrast to the original white stucco and faux half-timbering Tudor-style exterior.

In total, there was about $300,000 in furniture and other assets, which gave Gary a deduction of $30,000 from the amount owed on his ordinary federal income tax. The Economic Recovery Tax Act of 1981 reduced the top tax rate from 70 to 50 percent. Still, Gary would surrender half of his ordinary income to the government but for depreciation, which according to the Internal Revenue Service (IRS) is "an annual allowance for the wear and tear, deterioration, or obsolescence of the property." This includes both the structure and its contents (furniture and equipment). A deduction for depreciation can be claimed for five years.

"I really got in the hotel business for tax shelter," Gary explained. He accumulated enough cash—which he didn't have to give to the government—to put down $100,000 on each property.

Now Gary owned two businesses, both profitable. The hotels were not big money makers—yet. Gary would soon perfect the art of cutting costs while improving quality. In the early 1980s, he was beginning to learn how the hospitality industry works. To that end, he attended regional and national lodging conventions where he could quiz successful hotel owners and officials from various brands, such as Choice Hotels (Comfort Inn, Comfort Suites, Econo

Lodge, Quality Inn) and Super 8 Motels, which was founded in Aberdeen, South Dakota, 175 miles southwest of Fargo, in 1972. Super 8 is currently the largest budget hotel chain worldwide.

Gary's two Super 8 hotels turned a small profit since the one in Valley City had only 30 rooms and the Devils Lake hotel had 39 rooms. He could have kept buying local hotels as his need for tax shelters grew. But to accumulate one or even two such properties per annum was definitely not doing something big in Gary's view, especially since these were only marginally profitable. He sensed an opportunity for much more—and he was driven towards it by an inner engine that was configured to keep accelerating.

―――――――――――

As a young boy, Gary lay in bed at night planning on becoming a professional baseball player. By the time he reached high school, he realized he didn't have enough talent. Gary's childhood dream did not die, however, but was transformed.

"Then I wanted to do something on a large scale that would catapult me up to where a Major League Baseball player would be," he recalled.

Perhaps he should have said, "to where an entire Major League Baseball team would like to be."

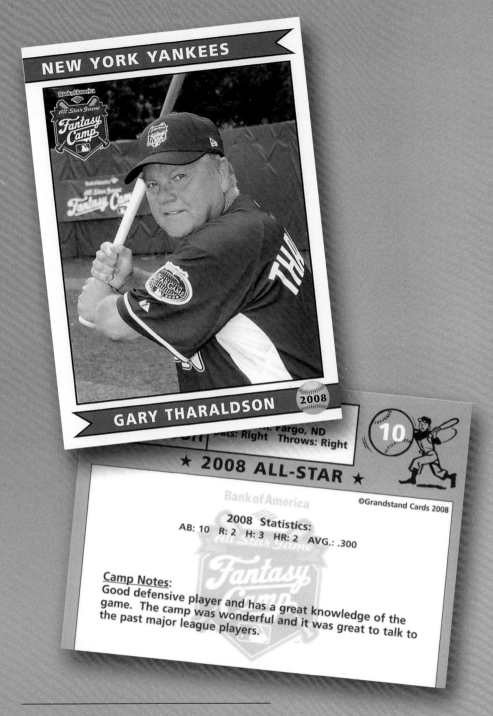

NEW YORK YANKEES

GARY THARALDSON

2008

Fargo, ND
Bats: Right   Throws: Right

★ **2008 ALL-STAR** ★

10

Bank of America   ©Grandstand Cards 2008

2008 Statistics:
AB: 10   R: 2   H: 3   HR: 2   AVG.: .300

Fantasy

<u>Camp Notes:</u>
Good defensive player and has a great knowledge of the game. The camp was wonderful and it was great to talk to the past major league players.

Gary participated in a fantasy baseball camp in New York City. The camp included tickets for the 2008 All-Star Game at Yankee Stadium and then a game against former Yankees, including Tommy John, the next day at the stadium.

CHAPTER FIVE

Strategic Thinking

You've got to be very careful if you don't
know where you are going, because you
might not get there.

Yogi Berra

The most dangerous strategy
is to jump a chasm in two leaps.

Benjamin Disraeli

BY THE END OF 1982, Gary made a monumental decision: Instead of buying hotels, he would build hotels. What happened as a result made peers such as Bruce White call Gary a "genius." White is the founder, Chairman and CEO of White Lodging, a top hospitality company whose portfolio includes 170 select-service, extended-stay and full-service hotels in 21 states.

Although it's obvious that Gary is highly intelligent, he would never agree to the label "genius." But then, historically, true geniuses never call themselves so. Most of what Gary does requires average to above-average intelligence to imitate, but not membership in American Mensa (although Gary would belong if tested). In fact, Gary makes the point that, "I kept things simple so anyone can learn what I'm doing."

IQ and genius, however, are not synonymous. Throughout history, there have been many highly intelligent artists, writers, philosophers, politicians and so on who are not considered geniuses.

While geniuses possess high intelligence and other gifts in abundance, there is something unique about their accomplishments. "Talent is like the marksman who hits a target, which others cannot reach," wrote Arthur Schopenhauer, a 19th-century German philosopher. "Genius is like the marksman who hits a target, which others cannot see."

In that sense, there is the note of genius in Gary, albeit in a minor key. He did not change the way we view the physical world and propose radical new theories that reshaped science like Albert Einstein. Nor did Gary invent human nature as we view it today, as critic Harold Bloom attributed to Shakespeare. However, in the narrow arena of the hospitality industry, Gary initiated important innovations, created the best profit-making and empire-building template, and transformed the hotel franchise culture—both among franchisees and between franchisees and corporate hotel brands. In that world, White was right.

Remarkably, as White pointed out, Gary is also a man without pretense. "If you call him down-to-earth, that's unfair," said White, "because I think he's actually subterranean." Intelligence and achievement bred a deeper humility, rather than arrogance. Gary's head didn't get bigger as his net worth grew.

The best way to comprehend—and learn from—the trajectory of Gary's career is to understand strategic thinking. Gary was never trained as a strategic thinker, nor even read a book dedicated to the art and science of strategy. Instinctively—and by the uncommon ability to learn quickly from experience—he grasped the essentials and implemented them brilliantly, thereby achieving extraordinary success.

"I'm more of a Tony-Robbins-type guy for reading," Gary said, "but what I think about is how to make every aspect of my business better and about how to find the best sites ever. They just don't fall on your lap."

Strategy is "the intellectual framework guiding individuals and/or organizations towards sustained success," according to USAF Col. (Ret) John A. Warden III. He is "one of America's premier strategic thinkers," wrote USAF (Ret) Perry Smith, author of *Rules and Tools for Leaders* and *Assignment: Pentagon, How to Excel in a Bureaucracy.* Col. Warden was the leading theorist of military air power and the architect of Operation Desert Storm's air campaign, as chronicled in *John Warden and the Renaissance of American Air Power* by John Andreas Olsen (Potomac Books, 2007).

In fact, in *The Air Campaign: John Warden and the Classical Airpower* (Air University Press, 1999), historian David R. Mets suggested that Col. Warden should be considered among the world's leading airpower theorists, along with RAF Marshal Hugh Trenchard, known as the father of the U.K.'s Royal Air Force, and Brig. Gen. William "Billy" Mitchell, known as the father of the U.S. Air Force.

After retiring from the military in 1995, Col. Warden founded Venturist, Inc., which provides strategic consulting services to businesses, including major corporations and other organizations. Col. Warden also established the Prometheus Academy, an intensive five-day seminar that immerses leaders and managers in strategic thinking as applied to their organizational objectives.

I (the author) met Col. Warden in 2012 when we served together on the board of the Reilly Center for Science, Technology and Values at the University of Notre Dame. The following May, I attended the Prometheus Academy seminar, which was a highly enlightening experience. Afterwards, Col. Warden and I wrote several articles about international security and military strategy for Forbes.com.

Strategic thinking involves four key aspects:

Gary Tharaldson talks with business students in 2016 at the Gary Tharaldson School of Business on the University of Mary's Bismarck campus, which was constructed and endowed through Gary's generosity. The Tharaldson School of Business promotes ethical values throughout its curriculum, dedicated to the belief that business can be a force for good.

1. **Future Picture:** useful, durable objective(s) with measures.

2. **Target Selection:** to create the conditions necessary to realize strategic objective(s).

3. **Campaign Timeframe:** adequate to achieving success, while depriving the opponent of the ability to react

4. **Exit Plan:** to transition effectively from success or failure with finesse.

As Col. Warden illustrates in his consulting practice, public talks and writings, including his book *Winning in FastTime: Harness the Competitive Advantage of Prometheus in Business and Life* (Venturist Publishing, 2001), determining one's strategic goal(s) and appropriate tactics begins with "scoping the environment." When Gary built his first hotels as a novice in the hospitality industry, he saw the need for new hotels in the area. In small to medium-sized towns and cities throughout North Dakota and the Midwest, there were few hotels, and existing properties were showing their age. Also, high interest rates and a sluggish economy stymied other potential developers.

"People wanted clean, convenient and modern places to stay back then," Gary remarked, "and few were available."

It was (and, for the most part, remains) true that Midwesterners typically weren't interested in expensive, full-service hotels. They consider these "too spendy." North Dakota and similar states had agriculturally based economies and low-income levels. The median income in North Dakota declined 9.4 percent during the 1980s to rank 44th in the nation in the 1990 census. South Dakota ranked 47th, and Kansas and Iowa ranked 30th and 37th, respectively.

"Gary's timing was superb," said Rick Larson in an interview. Larson has worked with Gary as one of his building developers for the past 24 years. "The motels and hotels in small cities back then were getting old and rundown."

Timing is not merely a matter of luck. Discovering improvements to the blacksmithing trade was far less advantageous in 1920, as Model-T Fords were flowing off assembly lines, than in 1820, when horses were still essential to transportation. Timing is largely a matter of observation—of scoping the environment—to see what product and services, or what invention or innovation, is needed or will be needed in the near future.

By the 1830s, for example, trains and railways were starting to appear, and the second half of the 19th century was characterized by the rapid development of railroads traversing the continent. Most of the fortunes made at the time were connected to railways directly or indirectly—and made by people who opened their eyes to seize new opportunities.

As soon as Gary got a taste of the hospitality business in 1982, he knew he could do something big. In insurance, he could do something comfortable, but he could never compete with major insurance companies that write billions of dollars in new policies every year. Perhaps he could have built up his firm to become the top insurance agency in the state. A worthy goal—but not enough. It wasn't that Gary was vain or seeking material opulence, nor was he seeking attention or adulation. Rather, he felt an inner calling. As Jesus said, "Many are called but few are chosen." Why? Because few choose.

Gary's Future Picture involved building and running many hotels. Every few years, he set goals for how many hotels—sometimes with humorous results.

In October 1982, Gary opened the first hotel he ever built, a Super 8 in Beulah, North Dakota, about 75 miles northwest of Bismarck. His second hotel, also a Super 8, opened in December 1983 in Kearney, Nebraska.

In March 1984, Gary interviewed Doug Dobmeier to work in Valley City as the bookkeeper for the hotels. During their conversation, Gary told Doug that he wanted to build 25 hotels by the end of 1987. Doug went home that evening and told his wife and parents at dinner.

"That's crazy," his wife responded.

"Yeah, I don't think we can ever get that big," Doug replied.

Even so, Dobmeier took the position and soon became the de facto head of hotel operations. Gary recalled that Dobmeier wasn't very competent at operations in the beginning, but Gary didn't know enough to realize this. Together, however, they learned through experience, and Doug officially became the Vice President of Operations in the mid-1990s, overseeing about 350 hotels.

Over the next three and a half years, Gary built 15 hotels, including 11 Super 8s (in Kansas, North Dakota, Minnesota, Nebraska, Kentucky and Arkansas), two Comfort Inns (Nebraska) and one Econo Lodge (North Dakota).

Gary fell short of his strategic goal by 10 hotels—the last time he would do so.

It should be noted that a strategic goal, or the Future Picture in Warden's terms, is like a guiding light or a beacon that illuminates one's desired destination. But it doesn't show how to get there. Endeavoring to build 25 hotels is obviously a measurable goal, but the question of how to construct more than seven per year remained open. The "how" is a tactical concern.

This difference is often overlooked in strategic planning. Mistaking tactics for strategy can be fatal for any endeavor. Consider the Vietnam War, during which American armed forces successfully executed a wide range of tactics over many years. Tactical success was almost perfect, yet the U.S. lost the war precisely because tactics were not aligned properly with a coherent Future Picture. Focusing on tactical success without proper alignment is like jumping on one's horse and heading "madly off in all directions," as humorist (and economist) Stephen Leacock famously put it.

The future that Gary was designing, however, involved more than merely building and owning as many hotels as possible. He also wanted to marry the best of quantity and quality in the endeavor. As chronicled on Tharaldson Hospitality Management's website, Gary "wrote down that simple original vision on a piece of paper in 1982. It consisted of the single goal of growing the business by enhancing the hotel visitor experience. We would focus on raising the performance of our hotels through the constant pursuit of three main actions: superior quality, superior service and superior function." Gary's emphasis on quality would also extend throughout the construction process. He built hotels that he intended to run for decades.

Even so, quality was something Gary and his company grew into. The buildings were well structured, but, for example "landscaping didn't even exist for us back in the early days," he said. "We paved right up to the building and put some parking blocks there so people wouldn't hit the building, and painted the blocks yellow. I always joked that our landscaping was the yellow paint."

Still, Gary's strategic objective was and remains: to build and run as many hotels as possible, as efficiently as possible and with the highest quality possible. When Gary strayed from this Future Picture, he made mistakes and jeopardized his business, as the reader will see in Chapter Eleven. When he returned to dedicating his financial and intellectual resources to this objective, as the reader will also see—when Gary "stuck to his knitting"—he resumed his almost magical dance with success.

———————————

There are many reasons why strategy and tactics misalign. The most pervasive is expressed in what has become axiomatic among management gurus and CEOs: culture eats strategy for breakfast—and for lunch and dinner. Organizations tend to become bureaucratic and therefore sclerotic. Executives and managers become more concerned with self-preservation and process than with responding innovatively to changing circumstances, to client needs and especially to new strategies.

Strategy must be embraced by all levels in any business from the CEO to hourly employees, Warden emphasized, or it will almost certainly fail. Instinctively, Gary kept his company lean in terms of the number and size of development and management teams. He both interacted personally with his key people, and empowered them to execute effectively and to make appropriate tactical decisions—according to his strategic goal, in which everyone was immersed.

———————————

Although Gary fell 40 percent short of reaching his first short-term goal, he hadn't failed to meet his long-term or meta-strategic goal, as stated above. However, the mini-goal failure brought the fourth part of strategic thinking into play—the exit plan. By definition, reaching a strategic goal constitutes an exit point. In general, just as often (or more so) as one achieves success, one falls short of reaching a goal. Either way, the exit point provides an opportunity—and usually, the necessity—to reconsider the strategic goal.

In this case, Gary felt far more invigorated by succeeding at building 15 hotels, which were turning a profit, than discouraged by not reaching 25 hotels. The experience taught him how to build, and he believed, as a result, that constructing 25 hotels in the next three years was a paltry objective. Gary would transition towards a much greater goal. He would work out how to build at least that many in a year, which was an outrageous strategic goal—for someone else. No private builder had ever attempted to build anywhere near that many hotels in such a short period.

"There are not many people with the passion and the ability to do things," Gary recounted. "I don't want to say I'm different; I know I'm different. It's all about passion."

While Gary's strategic meta-goal would remain in place for many years, he made shorter-term strategic goals every three to five years.

As Dobmeier said, "Gary was a risk-taker, but a very calculated risk-taker who always had faith that he was going to get things done right."

"Great leaders always seem to embody two seemingly disparate qualities," wrote John C. Maxwell in *The 21 Irrefutable Laws of Leadership*. "They are both highly visionary and highly practical."

CHAPTER SIX

The Thinker, the Doer & the Game

I skate to where the puck
is going to be, not where
it has been.

Wayne Gretsky

Remember, diamonds are
only lumps of coal that
stuck to their jobs.

B.C. Forbes

MANY CHALLENGES and obstacles are involved in building a single hotel, let alone building several and then many hotels simultaneously. As well as predictable issues, such as delays getting building permits, unpredictable problems can threaten reaching objectives.

For example, Gary was forced to refinance his Super 8 in Kearney, Nebraska, at the end of 1985 to get $300,000 to help pay off construction liens on five new hotels. Unexpectedly, one of Gary's building contractors took his money to finance other projects and then failed to pay many of the subcontractors on Gary's projects.

Gary also sold several cars he'd paid off to raise another $20,000 to help relieve the debts. And Gary borrowed $35,000 from his father and brother Rodney to pay off the remainder of the construction liens. By this time, Gary's parents were living in St. Paul, Minnesota, and his father was doing better as a masonry worker. Rodney had moved to Albert Lea, Minnesota, about 95 miles south of St. Paul, and was working as a meat cutter. Borrowing money from family members was not done lightly since they had few financial resources at the time.

Gary was determined to pay the loans back quickly, first to the bank and then to family. As soon as he learned of the construction liens, he met with his bankers and promised to pay off the liens within three months. They were very pleased to see him do exactly what he said.

This was both a matter of principle and a deft tactical move.

———————————

To understand what makes tactical sense, let's recall the second phase of Col. Warden's strategic thinking process: targeting for success. The basic question here is, where, among challenges and obstacles, does one choose to focus one's resources and in what order?

In war, for example, the enemy would have troops, weapons installations, airfields, airplanes, ships and so on. Although one might want to create the impression of attacking all assets simultaneously, this would likely be impractical, if not impossible. More importantly, this might not be necessary.

The strategic objective in Gulf War I was not to annihilate Iraqi forces but to force Iraq out of Kuwait with minimal casualties to both sides and to civil-

Gary with General Norman Schwarzkopf at a Choice Hotels International Annual Convention in the mid-1990s.

ians, and minimal damage to infrastructure. A typical "pound and ground" military campaign would have reduced Iraq to rubble and cost an estimated 20,000 Coalition and mostly American lives.

Gen. Norman Schwarzkopf, who was in charge of Operation Desert Storm, turned to Col. Warden to find a more viable strategy. One of the key transformative elements Col. Warden brought to military strategy was to conceive of "the enemy as a system composed of numerous subsystems." In business, the "enemy" would be the marketplace, competitors and even internal systems and/or personnel.

The question then is, how does one leverage this system to do what one wants or to allow one to achieve what one wants? Company A does not need to destroy competing companies. In fact, this could be counterproductive. Microsoft and Apple have dominated the computer world for decades, appealing to different customers and thereby establishing two main sectors in the computing marketplace. This symbiotically competitive relationship has forced other competitors to play by their rules or go out of business. If Apple folded tomorrow, that would create an opening for another major player that might not only claim Apple's market share but eventually threaten Microsoft's primacy, too.

Gulf War I's air campaign began at 2:00 a.m. AST (Arab Standard Time) on January 17, 1991. Col. Warden was in the basement of the Pentagon in his Checkmate Division watching the air attack on cable TV. He was sitting with Don B. Rice, Secretary of the Air Force, Maj. Gen. Robert M. Alexander, director of plans, Office of the Deputy Chief of Staff for Plans and Operations, USAF Headquarters, and several of the other officers who had been a part of the planning effort.

The TV coverage—termed a contemporary demonstration of "shock and awe" (or rapid dominance)—was broadcast to a worldwide audience. Seeing strategically important infrastructure blown up in real time with pinpoint accuracy was thrilling. But the most important targets were hit just after 3:00 a.m. AST and involved no pyrotechnics. Instead, military leaders and viewers saw the lights go out across Baghdad and Iraq like illuminated dominoes tumbling one after the other into a black hole.

"It's over," Col. Warden jumped up and declared. "There is nothing that the Iraqis can do to stop us now."

By understanding the enemy as a system, Col. Warden saw that the enemy's actions depended on electricity. Once Coalition fighter planes took out Iraq's electrical grid, its forces were rendered blind and the collapse of Iraq's military system was inevitable.

To shut down the grid without permanent damage, a special cruise missile was deployed that released thousands of electrically conductive fibers over Iraqi power stations, which created multiple short circuits and rapid shutdown. The Iraqis didn't have the technical capability to remove the fibers. But after the war, the fibers were quickly removed and the electrical grid functioned again. This scenario was part of the Future Picture for Iraq that Col. Warden included in the battle plan ("Instant Thunder"), which he presented to Gen. Norman Schwarzkopf, Commander-in-Chief of U.S. Central Command.

The point of the above anecdote regarding Gary is to show that in business, as in war, it's crucial to view the marketplace, competitors and one's own organizations as systems in order to determine how best to leverage them for the desired effect.

Paying off the construction liens quickly, as noted above, was a "deft tactical move" because this helped Gary build a positive relationship with bankers. As with most business ventures, access to capital is the largest hurdle, especially in the early years. Bankers provide that access in the form of loans and lines of credit. Financial resources, if used properly, are essential to any plan to affect the marketplace, which is the external system confronting an entrepreneur.

The other solution for a businessman without huge cash reserves involved taking on investing partners. Gary made a personal and business decision not to pursue this option. He calculated that the upside of having partners—access to more funds to invest in his business—was outweighed by the complications that would come with negotiating terms with partners. He did not want to do all the work and then have to split the profits with a partner who did nothing but invest or worse, set difficult conditions. Gary values his autonomy highly and makes decisions quickly, both of which would likely be compromised by partners.

The system Gary planned to change was the economy (budget to mid-priced limited- or select-service) sector of the lodging industry. He would also soon move into building extended-stay hotels and seek to become a major player in that sector of the hospitality marketplace. Without partners, Gary needed to turn to banks for access to enough capital to achieve his goals. The 1980s and early to mid-1990s, however, were plagued by a sluggish economy and high interest rates on loans. It was costly and often difficult to secure bank loans.

But, as Gary observed, "Banks still needed to make loans. That is their business." To get banks on board, he needed to show them that his hotels were profitable soon after opening, that profits were steady and that his hotels

"*As long as the Interstate is the highway supporting our society, economy, and national security, it will forever need to be the beneficiary of our attention and investment. The ribbon cuttings will never end!*" – Dan McNichol in *The Roads That Built America*

made money in bad economic times as well as good ones.

Turning a profit was not only the prime necessary condition to staying in business, it was the prime precondition to growth, to seizing the immense opportunity Gary perceived in the hospitality industry.

To understand the breadth of this opportunity, one must comprehend the context. Emerging from World War II, a sixth of all American workers were involved in manufacturing automobiles. In 1950, there were only about 25 million cars on the road, many of which were limping along if not completely broken down. The focus of wartime factories had been producing military parts and vehicles.

As industry retooled for peacetime, the public's appetite for new vehicles was voracious. Eight million cars rolled off assembly lines in 1950. Within a decade, there were 62 million cars and 12 million trucks on the road. Traffic congestion became an acute problem, exacerbated by the suburbanization of the growing middle class.

In response, President Dwight D. Eisenhower signed the Federal-Aid Highway Act in June 1956. By the 1980s, most of the 46,871-mile Interstate Highway System was built, and there were 121.6 million cars and 1.4 million trucks traversing these new roads.

"To understand America, you must understand highways," Robert Samuelson wrote in the Washington Post in 1986. "In this past century, these masochistic marvels have—along with telephones, televisions and jet planes—reshaped American culture."

Gary understood exactly how highways and automobiles were changing the country. And he saw clearly what was lagging in development: new hotels along the interstates for travelers to stay overnight or for extended periods for business or personal visits.

There were countless places to build in the Midwest, and land in most urban centers was not expensive. This posed the problem, not quite of "insurmountable opportunity" (as usually, but not definitively, attributed to Walt Kelly, the "Pogo" comic strip creator), but of exactly where—out of anywhere—to build. Pick the wrong spot and occupancy rates will fail to reach profitability for the venture, or competitors will build in the best locations and dominate the market.

In the restaurant business, it has become axiomatic that the three keys to success are: location, location, location. Obviously, the quality of the food and service matter greatly too, but the wrong location can be fatal to an eating establishment. This was especially true in the hotel business in the seemingly prehistoric era prior to cell phones and GPS.

Today's traveler can easily perform an Internet search for local hotels near his or her destination and then can readily be directed turn-by-turn to even an obscure spot. But in the 1980s and '90s, it was imperative for hotels to be situated near interstate highways and main urban routes—and to be clearly visible from those roads. If a traveler had trouble finding the hotel where his or her reservation had been made, that traveler would likely pull into another hotel along the roadway.

Targeting for success, for profits, in Gary's industry involves site location first and foremost. To find a site for a new hotel in the early years, Gary—often accompanied by Dobmeier in the early 1980s and then Roger Swahn (who attended college with Gary and started working for him at his insurance agency) until 1994—hopped in the company Ford Taurus with a set of maps and started driving. They did not head down county roads or side streets. They were seeking not merely obvious sites but the most obvious locations in the literal sense: visible from interstate highways and near an exit at the intersection of another interstate or major roadway.

For example, the Super 8 in Burnsville, Minnesota, which Gary opened in October 1986, sits near the fork of an interstate highway: I-35E goes into St. Paul and I-35 W runs into Minneapolis.

Similarly, the five hotels (one Econo Lodge, three Comfort Inns and one Fairfield Inn) that Gary built in Fargo from 1985 to 1992 are located along one of the two interstates cutting through the city, or at the intersection of these main arteries.

Gary and Dobmeier or Swahn researched city directories and newspapers and asked people for information about existing hotels. Gary and his business companion would check into a local hotel and quiz the clerk on duty and the manager. Since Gary was always friendly and unassuming, questions about room rates, occupancy levels and area demographics were usually answered in full. At 5'8", Gary doesn't seem intimidating, although certainly not a wimp. He weighs about 180 pounds and carries himself more like the halfback who will block for a teammate than the linebacker trying to smash an opponent into the turf. In his polo shirt (usually without the more-costly alligator) and khakis, Gary hardly looked like an aspiring millionaire, let alone a multi- and then mega-millionaire.

At the time, information about local income levels, spending and travel patterns, and future housing, retail and office development was not readily available online. Yet Gary had to assess these factors to determine the most viable hotel sites—not merely for the next few years but for decades. He was not building his portfolio for the short term. Selling properties was always an option and sometimes the best move, but he wanted to own and operate as many as possible for the long term. Also, selling hotels with a clearly profitable future eased the transaction and attracted the highest bids.

"We counted cars in hotel parking lots in the early days to know exactly what the occupancy was at hotels in areas we were thinking of," Gary recalled with a smile. "Site selection is the fun part of the business." It's analogous to winning at sports, and Gary loves to win. Site selection is an adventure, and certainly more so in the 1980s and early 1990s, when research was as hands-on as it was serendipitous.

"Site selection is a function of the local market," said Gary. As well as building along interstates, he built near shopping malls. Prior to online buying, almost all shopping occurred in stores, and by the 1980s, malls increasingly dominated the retail sales market. Also, mall developers located new retail hubs in carefully researched areas regarding local income levels, housing developments, office buildings, and future residential and commercial projects.

Dobmeier joked often that they were really "mall chasers."

They were also college chasers, office and industrial park chasers, airport chasers, and middle- to upper-middle-class demographic chasers. The proximity of one or more of these enhanced the potential site's value.

Through experience, Gary and his development staff formulated four criteria regarding site location in the mid-1980s:

1. Urban centers with more than 35,000 residents.

2. Proximity to interstate highways: visible from the highway and near an exit.

3. Presence of a college and/or university.

4. Proximity to a shopping mall(s), office building(s) and/or industrial park(s), and/or airports.

Not all of these site criteria had to be satisfied, and in fact it was rare to satisfy all of them simultaneously. The population at these locations ranged from 7,700 in Coralville, Iowa, to 314,000 in Omaha, Nebraska. Some urban centers might have seemed too small at first glance, but Coralville, for example, borders Iowa City, which had almost 60,000 residents when Gary built a Comfort Inn there in 1989. Iowa City also hosts the University of Iowa. Major universities create hospitality needs, especially at the beginning of the school year, graduation and on home football game weekends. The Iowa Hawkeyes play at Kinnick Stadium, less than two miles from the Comfort Inn.

Sometimes Gary picked the wrong site, which helped prove the efficacy of the site criteria. For example, he built a Comfort Inn in Wahpeton, North

Dakota, which opened in 1989. It never did very well, nor could it have in a city of 8,600 people that isn't situated near or between major urban centers. In retrospect, "I shouldn't have built in Wahpeton," Gary said, adding, "and the same for Jamestown, which did OK but nothing great. I was better off building in larger towns on the interstate." Jamestown, North Dakota, had about 15,500 residents in 1991, when Gary's Comfort Inn opened there.

"In small towns, there's too much land," Gary explained. "What happens is somebody is going to come in behind you and beat you up."

Gary built his last hotel in North Dakota in 1992. "At 60,000 to 70,000 people," he said, "we started hitting the sweet spot." Several cities in the state would qualify, but his answer to the question he's often asked locally, "Why does everybody build in Fargo?," explains it: "I say, 'Because they can. You can build all the way to Casselton if you want, and franchises are coming now with new brands all the time.'"

Gary was very quick "to pull the trigger," as Dobmeier attested, if he liked a site. In fact, he prized premium locations so much he would spend an extra $100,000 to $150,000, which was about 10 percent of construction costs in the 1980s, to get a desired site.

Gary was "Mr. Frugal," Dobmeier recalled with a good-natured laugh. Not only did they travel in non-descript, aging American-made sedans, they shared a hotel room. When Gary was building hotels at a furious pace and flying to check out potential sites, he would share a room with his pilot.

"One of his favorite lunch places is Red Lobster," Dobmeier said. "For years, Gary would order the shrimp entrée with one of his coworkers and then split it."

Still, he was not cheap. Gary provided the capital for everything his development, construction and operations people needed to do their jobs well. He also paid well and went to extraordinary lengths to ensure that everyone, from housekeeper to manager, ended up better off financially than if they had worked elsewhere.

His frugality went hand in hand with the construction and operational efficiencies he developed that enabled him to grow his companies so quickly

Gary's first house in Fargo, ND, (102 Prairiewood Drive) after moving from Valley City in 1989. Gary lived there in 1990 and '91 with his wife Linda and their three children: Michael, Michelle and Matthew.

and to such a phenomenal size. Gary's family lived well but not ostentatiously. To this day, Gary still buys his clothes at stores like J.C. Penney.

His one indulgence was driving a luxury car for personal use—in the 1990s, a Lincoln Continental or a Cadillac. He didn't drive a more expensive S-Class Mercedes Benz, 7 Series BMW or, the "spendy" gods forbid, a Rolls Royce, which he could have afforded by then.

Instead of spending on himself, Gary poured as much revenue as possible back into growing the business. This did not go unnoticed.

"My message to our employees was, 'Look at this guy. He's reinvesting all of his money back into us. So with that, there are going to be opportunities,'" said Dobmeier. They saw that, as Gary continued to build."

Clearly, Gary wasn't scraping off the profits but maximizing revenues for everyone's benefit. As a result, many employees stayed for decades and company culture grew strong.

Once the right site was located, the real work began: how to build and run the hotel at maximum profit, and how to do so while building dozens at a time. Instead of adopting the "Boxer syndrome," the typical approach to challenges among business owners, Gary did the opposite. Boxer is the horse in George Orwell's *Animal Farm* who believes that any problem can be resolved by working harder. *Animal Farm* was published exactly two months before Gary's birth. Coincidence or not, Gary figured out at the beginning of his career that working smarter, not merely longer hours, is the key to success.

Gary developed a personal work protocol he coined the "25/40 rule." Instead of spending 80 hours a week at the office and visiting his growing number of hotels in a frenzied quest to improve processes, he decided to spend only 25 hours a week at the office or in the field. And he spent another 40 hours a week thinking about ways to improve his business ventures.

"Most businesspeople are really busy, and the temptation for most is to work harder and harder," Gary said. "I choose not to be occupied all the time, but my mind is working. I think strategy, I think about cutting costs and I think about making the company better without increasing expenses much. This way helps me perform at my best."

There seems to be solid scientific grounds for Gary's experience. A recent study by researchers at the Melbourne Institute of Applied Economic and Social Research showed that for people over 40 years of age, working more than 25 hours per week "cause[s] psychological stress, which potentially damage[s] cognitive functioning." Gary turned 40 years of age in 1985, just as his hotel career was taking off.

His brainstorms didn't occur in a vacuum. He went meticulously through every line item in the development and operating budgets to determine "how to keep our labor and other costs down so that we would still provide a high quality of service to our guests and become a profitable company."

Watching Gary at work is like watching a chess master playing chess—speed chess, that is. Gary is both the pensive general meditating over the board and the captain on the field of battle executing the strategy. As well, it would be fair to say that as his staff gained experience, Gary let the rooks, knights and bishops make their own moves. They were sufficiently well-trained, and Gary was always present or available for consultation via pager and, beginning in the 1990s, by email and cell phone.

Out of this cauldron of precise analysis and vivid imagination emerged numerous innovations and efficiencies, which eventually became industry standards. They make total sense in retrospect, but they were radical departures from what hotel developers and management companies were doing at the time.

"The thing that's really neat about Gary is that he has the foresight to see things others don't," said Aimee Fyke, Gary's COO. "He's made mistakes; he's not immune. But Gary has gotten a lot more things right than wrong."

By 1988, Gary was overseeing hotel construction in seven states (North Dakota, South Dakota, Iowa, Kansas, Minnesota, Illinois and Indiana). Since Gary was familiar with construction after working on projects with his father and then during his college years, he operated as his own contractor, with one or more professionals such as Don Cowers and Larry Madson functioning as the de facto general contractor or project manager(s), depending on how many hotels were under construction. He used the same crews, which travelled from site to site, for framing and for telephone and other electronics installations. Gary also experimented with moving his own crane and excavation crew from site to site but found that it was better to rent equipment locally and use local crews for excavation and other construction stages. As these local crews proved their value, Gary would use them repeatedly.

"We were novices trying to figure all this out as we went," Gary recalled. "We experimented with logistics about moving crews around." What worked Gary kept and what didn't work was discarded.

Although a "novice," Gary was executing a bold plan, the first in the lodging industry, to become a vertically integrated development and operations company. In 1984, he established Tharaldson Enterprises, Inc., as a shell company overseeing all operations, which fell into four business divisions: Tharaldson Development, which took care of site location and construction; Tharaldson Property Management, Inc., which managed the hotels after construction or after purchase; Tharaldson Properties, which managed the company's two corporate office buildings in Fargo; and Midwest Marketing, which was Gary's insurance agency that was still receiving renewal fees.

Tharaldson Enterprises took care of negotiating with vendors, procurement (including FF&E—that is, furniture, fixtures and equipment not connected to the building), landscaping, phone systems, marketing—all aspects of building and running hotels. This enabled Gary to cut costs—saving about $80,000 on construction costs and then $25,000 to $30,000 per hotel per year in operations—and ensure quality.

"If you accumulate all this information, you know you are going to get 120 to 130 percent," Gary said, meaning 20 to 30 percent above the local market's average occupancy.

Gary implemented three important design innovations into the construction of his hotels. As early as in the first hotel Gary built in Beulah, North Dakota, in 1982, he located the laundry room behind the front desk at new hotels. This enabled the night clerk, who had little else to keep him or her busy, to do the laundry when utility costs were lower. This move saved Gary about $7,000 annually at each hotel since he was able to eliminate the need for either a full-time or several part-time positions.

By 1987, when Gary stopped selling insurance part-time, the laundry room innovation was saving about $98,000 per year at 14 hotels. This increased to $1.6 million per year in 1996 and then to more than $2 million per year by century's end. As Gary started building larger hotels, at 90 to 105 rooms, it became clear that putting the laundry room behind the front desk was impractical. He built several hotels that size in the late 1990s with the laundry innovation, which didn't work well since the night manager was needed more often at the front desk as the number of guests increased. In 2001, the last of Gary's hotels with laundry facilities behind the front desk was built.

"In North Dakota, Gary was all by himself and didn't have people telling him he couldn't do things his way," said Bruce White, the head of White Lodging. He met Gary in the early 1980s, when they both got into the hospitality business, and they became good friends. "He wasn't held hostage by other people's thoughts. Instead of looking at how things are done, he starts from ground zero with a clean sheet of paper." Basically, Gary had his "own laboratory" to experiment in.

Magnate's brain is busy, not his office

• Lodging dynasty's owner spends 25 hours a week at work, 40 hours thinking of new ways to make profit

BY PETER SMOLOWITZ
Associated Press

Associated Press

Gary Tharaldson (front), owner of more than 235 motels and hotels, originated the idea of night clerks doing laundry in a room behind the front desk.

FARGO, N.D.: Gary Tharaldson says he works only about 25 hours a week at his office, but he spends about 40 hours thinking of ways to make his business better.

"A lot of businessmen are really busy people," Tharaldson says. "I choose not to be busy, but my mind is working. It's a process where you try to be the best you can possibly be."

His thoughts have helped Tharaldson Enterprises make $50 million a year, and have helped make its 51-year-old owner and president worth about $575 million. Forbes magazine calls Tharaldson the richest man in North Dakota.

Tharaldson grew up in the tiny town of Dazey in east-central North Dakota. The high school farmhand and Valley City State University grad tried teaching and selling life insurance before launching a lodging dynasty by opening a series of no-frills hotels and motels throughout the Midwest.

He now owns more than 235 hotels under 15 different brands, from Courtyard Mariotts to Super 8s, and aspires to add one new hotel every nine days.

"You always set goals, and that's always been one of my goals – to be the best," he said. "Money is just a measuring stick. It doesn't mean that much to me. The game is what I like."

One of his brainstorms was to put laundry rooms behind the front desk in his hotels. Doing laundry keeps his night clerks busy and saves him about $5,500 annually at each hotel – a total of roughly $1.25 million.

He pays the housekeepers who clean his 16,000 rooms by the suite cleaned, not by the hour, to save the company money and create a shorter workday for the staff.

"If we were paid by the hour, we'd lose money," says Anne Schneiter, head housekeeper at Fargo's Comfort Inn, who has been cleaning Tharaldson's rooms for nine years.

Tharaldson, who owns only one suit, which he seldom wears to work, says he has a relaxed, open-door policy with his workers, and can answer any company-related question within 30 seconds. The father of six children, from a newborn to a 28-year-old, Tharaldson offers a free stay on Thanksgiving and Christmas to people visiting hospitalized friends and families.

His business' size allows him to buy items wholesale, and he arranges

See BRAIN, Page F6

Gary in the laundry room behind the front desk—one of his signature innovations—at the Fairfield Inn in Fargo, ND.

"And what I find fascinating is that it's not like he's the classic amateur who just does things and doesn't really know how to do it right," White continued. "Gary does know how other people do it, but he just says, 'Well, that doesn't work well.' Then he has enough confidence to go out and do it differently."

Through inspiration and then trial and error, Gary determined what worked best in all aspects of lodging. "It's interesting to wonder whether, if Gary had grown up in Chicago or somewhere similar," White mused, "he would have ended up in the same place."

Creators, inventors and innovators often discover and create on the edges of society rather than at the center. Apple was born in the family garage of Steve Jobs' childhood home in Los Altos, California. Microsoft began operations humbly in Albuquerque, New Mexico. Gary grew up in Dazey, one of the most obscure small towns in the country. Beginning his business in Valley City wasn't much farther away from the edge of the known world. Then, while opening hotels across the Midwest, he didn't have to worry about negative reviews in national publications such as the New York Times or Travel+Leisure magazine. In fact, these venues still haven't taken notice of the man or his business accomplishments.

The second of Gary's design innovations involved putting corridors and the swimming pool inside the hotel. The classic motel placed entrances at each room's exterior, as in the photo below. For Gary, this made no more sense in northern parts of the country than building outdoor swimming pools there, which would make better skating rinks during the winter months. Exterior entrances greatly increased heating and cooling costs, and they were certainly not secure—as scores of Hollywood TV shows and films have illustrated.

From the start, Gary built hotels with indoor corridors on all floors and an indoor pool, which guests appreciated. This soon became the industry standard.

The most important design innovation Gary introduced was under-building his hotels. "Think small to grow big" articulates the mindset that powered much of Gary's success. Most brands in the Midwest, even in the economy class, were built from a template for 70 to 100 rooms. As Gary put it, "they were built for good times, but in down cycles, they had difficulty making money."

The hotel above, not a Tharaldson property, provides room access through exterior corridors. Studies and feedback indicate consumer preference for interior-corridor properties, driven largely by a greater sense of security.

They were simply too large for their markets and often ran at occupancy rates lower than the national average of 63 percent and 15 to 20 percent lower than the rate at Gary's hotels, which averaged between 75 and 85 percent. This translated immediately to the bottom line since these hotels cost more to build and run.

"It's about knowing the local market," he said. "Today we can get all the information from the Internet. Years ago, we would go into a market and figure out occupancy levels at hotels near a site and in the entire town. If hotels were typically at 100 rooms and they ran 60 percent full, then I would build a hotel around 60 rooms and run 80 to 90 percent occupancy. It's simple math, right?"

In the 1980s, the size of Gary's hotels ranged from 39 rooms in Beulah to 76 rooms in Omaha, Nebraska—according to the market. Beulah had 3,100 residents while Omaha had 325,000. In total, Gary built 37 hotels by the end of 1989 with 2,740 rooms. The average hotel size was 56 rooms.

The Beulah hotel was a Super 8, the best economy brand at the time in Gary's estimation. The Omaha hotel was a Comfort Inn, which was the next

Interior-corridor hotels, as at the Staybridge Suites in Columbus, Ohio, offer a more contemporary product, and enjoy consistent occupancy and average daily rate premiums versus exterior-corridor hotels.

step up in quality and, in Gary's view, the best brand in the economy/limited-service lodging sector.

Building smaller also allowed Gary to lower construction costs, borrow less per project and incur less debt service. Smaller properties also cost less to run and maintain, both as a physical plant and in terms of staff. A smaller hotel requires fewer people and, therefore, less compensation and benefits costs, even if these employees are paid more than at competing hotels.

Training costs are also lower as significantly less talent is needed. Staffing a hotel involves much more than finding warm bodies. Mastering all the tasks staff members must perform in real time, while interacting warmly and professionally with guests, requires a combination of talents and disposition lacking in many candidates—regardless of their level of formal education. Any company is far more likely to recruit, train and retain 10 desirable candidates than 20.

When Gary was asked in 2017 how he would start out today in the hotel industry, his advice was essentially the same: build small to grow big.

"Build a smaller property in a smaller market," Gary replied. "If you could raise two or three million dollars in equity today, you could do a $10 million property." The same Fairfield Inn that cost $27,000 per room (or per key) in 1992 costs $34,000 in 1998 and more than $73,000 today. (This is the construction cost, not the all-in cost—which includes land, architectural and engineering expenses and cost overruns—that is typically 25 percent higher.)

"Put the whole deal together," Gary advised. "Get it built, get it owned and get it running. Remember, you have to have enough capital to keep it running for three to six months. A new hotel doesn't make a penny until the doors open. While it's possible to get on the brand's reservation system before day one, it's difficult to pinpoint an exact opening date."

Even after building almost 500 hotels, Gary said with a dry laugh that, "we're still setting dates back all the time because of a city building department."

Building small allows the owner to have more cash in reserve to keep the enterprise afloat during unforeseen delays.

On the operations side, Gary and Dobmeier discovered obvious practical truths. "Our first hotels were ma-and-pa operations. We had a husband-and-wife management team who lived in an apartment at the hotel," said Dobmeier. These teams, however, were more the "any warm body" variety. Soon Dobmeier started recruiting professionals or at least candidates who could be trained to be proficient and please guests.

"I went out and got to know the people who were working for us," Dobmeier recalled. "Then we started putting systems processes in place from scratch and wrote manuals for front-desk procedures and so on."

"We focused a lot on the per-room cost of operating our hotels," Dobmeier said. "One important thing we did was clarify what general managers were responsible for. We cut their liability off at what we call our GHP, the Gross House Profit line." This included labor and other costs that could be controlled on site. "Below that was real estate taxes, insurance, franchise and maintenance fees and so on. That was stuff that Gary worked on."

Gary contemplating strategy at the Miller Lite Softball Tournament
in Fargo in June 1991.

As Gary examined line-item costs, he pondered ways to reduce labor expenses, which is the biggest non-fixed expenditure. Accordingly, he experimented with paying maids on a per-room basis rather than by the hour. In 1985, when this practice was initiated, the minimum hourly wage was $3.35 (which equates to $7.88 in 2017 dollars). Hard-working maids loved the innovation since they could earn 25 to 100 percent more.

At the same time, managers inspected the rooms, as well as bedding, hallways and common areas, to ensure results. On regular visits, both Dobmeier and Gary scrutinized the entire hotel, including the laundry room and other areas not open to guests.

Both Gary and Dobmeier were "sticklers on cleanliness," as Dobmeier put it. "I really am anal about it." This fit neatly into Gary's perception that what most travelers want most is a clean, quiet room with a good bed to get a restful night's sleep.

Gary saved 25 percent on housekeeping labor costs, which amounted to about $130 per room per year. In total, this saved about $365,000 in 1989 and then more than $2 million in 1997. Soon afterwards, however, Gary had to revert to paying maids by the hour. Changes in labor regulations created an "accounting nightmare," since his hotels had to ensure that all maids were earning at least minimum wage.

This shift troubled Gary since his best cleaning staff had to adjust to a significant loss of income. As the reader will see in Chapter Nine, Gary made a dramatic move to share the wealth his companies were generating with all employees, down to the janitors and cleaning maids.

Another labor-saving innovation involved scheduling the hotel managers to work the desk shift three times a week. At first this was merely a way to cut costs since this move eliminated three-fifths of a full-time position. Serendipitously, "we discovered that when the manager was at the front desk," Gary said, "we got better results, both in customer satisfaction and higher room rates, because the most qualified person was handling the guests." This saved each hotel $8,000 to $10,000 per year.

In the 1980s, very few motels or economy hotels offered breakfast. Full-service hotels operated (and still operate) restaurants on the premises that offer sit-down breakfast, as do some mid-level lodgings. But limited-service lodgings seldom even made coffee available back then. Gary believed it was very important to offer coffee and doughnuts to get people on the road in a positive mood—and to motivate return business.

Coffee and doughnuts soon necessitated the "doughnut report," which Dobmeier recalled with a healthy laugh. Gary wanted the managers to determine exactly how many doughnuts were being consumed every day and then buy accordingly. "Gary was making the point to his managers about knowing their business in detail, and about knowing how many guests you're going to have and so how many doughnuts you're going to need," Dobmeier related.

*An architectural rendering of the company headquarters building in Fargo, ND,
which Gary built and opened in time for the corporate office to move there in August
1989. The building, located on Frontage Road east of Interstate 29, is no longer
occupied by any of the Tharaldson companies.*

"In the head office, we used to laugh about the doughnut reports when the
managers sent them on those old fax machines."

Doughnuts and coffee cost 35 cents a room in the mid-1980s. Pennies
could be saved via the doughnut reports. As the number of Gary's hotels
grew, pennies turned into thousands of dollars, and then tens of thousands of
dollars per year.

However, Gary was not satisfied with coffee and doughnuts to start the
day. This offering soon evolved into continental breakfast. Per-room breakfast
costs increased rapidly as bacon and scrambled eggs became standard fare,
along with English muffins, fruit and yogurt. As the new century approached,
breakfast cost $3 per room at the 326 hotels Gary owned. Today, the cost is
$4 per room.

The doughnut report evolved, too, into sophisticated digital inventory
control and procurement programs. Saving just 10 cents per room per day—
no longer via doughnut reports but sophisticated online inventory control—
added up to about $775,000 per year in 2000.

Left to right, Michael, Matthew, Michelle and Gary Tharaldson at Michelle's wedding at Atonement Lutheran Church in Fargo, ND, on September 12, 1998.

Offering breakfast soon became an industry standard. Today, it would be difficult to find a limited-service or extended-stay hotel in the country that doesn't offer a complimentary breakfast of some variety.

Gary turned his cost-cutting genius to all facets of his business, from procurement to phone systems. In 1992, Bruce Thune installed the phone systems in the two Fairfield Inn & Suites that Gary built in Bismarck that year. This saved $6,000 to $8,000 per hotel, plus $100 per month in service charges for each property. Thune was then hired to install phone systems in all of Gary's hotels. Today, he still installs phones, as well as all electronic services, in Gary's properties. Current installations include Internet, high-speed security systems, cable TV, background music and the particular requirements of each brand—for example, interactive TV for Marriott brands. Thune's work saves Gary about $18,000 per hotel, plus $150 per month in service charges for each property.

To add to the bottom line before widespread, inexpensive cell phone

Gary, his parents and siblings at Michelle's wedding. Left to right (back row) Gary, Roger, Rodney; (front row) Delphine, Russel, June, Connie, Cleone.

usage, Gary charged each room 50 cents a day for unlimited local calls. This increased revenue by $15,000 per year per hotel, which added up to $4.8 million per year by the end of 1999.

The key to profitability, Gary often says, is not merely to sell rooms but to improve yield. Many competitors, he pointed out, achieve high occupancy rates but don't pay enough attention to costs and fail to grow their businesses nearly as quickly as Gary did. High profit margins enable debt service and operating costs to be covered, with enough cash left over to provide the equity for building new hotels.

Gary's wife Linda also contributed to the company's innovative tradition. She started working at the company head office in Valley City in 1988 and then moved with her husband and their family to Fargo in August 1989, when Gary set up headquarters in a new building he built near the intersection of Interstates 94 and 29. This was close to the two local hotels he owned then (an Econo Lodge and a Comfort Inn) and also near a second Comfort Inn, which he was building. At that time, Gary and Linda's eldest, Michael, was 19 years old and working as an entrepreneur. Michelle, 17, was a freshman at Moorhead State Community and Technical College in Moorhead, Minnesota, where she studied sales and marketing management. Matthew, 10, was entering 5th grade at the local public school.

Gary asked Linda to check over hotel invoices, and soon she was negotiating all the contracts with vendors. "She was a very smart businesswoman," he said. "Whatever Linda had to do, she would get it done. She was very good at it."

Linda came up with the notion to offer free hotel rooms on Thanksgiving and Christmas to people visiting hospitalized friends or family. The idea made sense since, as well as providing a service for people in need, the holidays are usually slow days in the hospitality business. It didn't hurt the company's public image either.

From 1988 through 2006, by which time most of Gary's hotels were sold, the company gave away 450 rooms a year.

Gary and Linda proved to be a great team in the office even after they divorced in 1991. Linda continued as head of procurement for both construction and operations until 1994, and she was also involved in hotel design and openings. As the Tharaldson Enterprises grew, she moved out of development and procurement to concentrate on marketing. In 1998, Linda signed a 20-year marketing consultant agreement.

As marketing head, she kept costs down to 1.25 percent of operating expenses, which is three to four times less than the industry standard. "We didn't use billboards because they were very expensive," Gary recalled. "With a good location, we would let the other hotels nearby advertise on billboards on the interstate and direct people to our exit. Then we'd pick 'em off because we always had the best hotel brands."

Also, Gary's emphasis on guest satisfaction created loyal customers who generate the best advertising, especially before Facebook: word of mouth.

Sometimes the best innovation involves not innovating. Gary began his career with Super 8 hotels, which provide neither room service nor restaurants. As he moved up the brand ladder, he stuck with this formula. "I don't need the headache of operating on-site restaurants," he said, since this would involve him in a completely different business that he didn't understand—nor wanted to.

Gary's vision remained clear: offer clean, comfortable rooms at affordable rates ($40 to $70 in the late 1980s and early 1990s) with top-notch service.

————————————

While Gary might be seen in contemporary terms as having a somewhat ADHD personality, he didn't allow this to gain sway over the vision of the future he was creating. Gary's mantra about keeping things simple is as much a shrewd insight into organizational productivity as it is a discipline.

Gary's capacity to "build incredible economies into the development of the project by focusing on building and operational efficiencies," as White put it, appealed to bankers who enabled Gary to transition from strategic thinking's second phase, in Col. Warden's conception, to the third phase: from target selection to campaigning to win.

Target selection primarily involved site and brand selection. Campaigning to win involves scaling up Gary's building and operating systems to dominate the marketplaces he chose to compete in. In short, Gary set a pace that no other developer could come close to matching, which gave him huge advantages in capturing opportunities—convincing local banks to back him.

CHAPTER SEVEN

The Gary Tharaldson Express

Capitalism is the only system
in the world founded on
credit and character.

Hubert Eaton

It's kind of fun to
do the impossible.

Walt Disney

FOR A LOST TRAVELER in the Sahara Desert or a drowning man or woman, water means everything. For an Olympic swimmer, it's a means to an end—critically essential, but not the goal per se. For a businessman, money is an enterprise's food and fuel, the means by which companies are built or broken. Money is everything for a business just getting off the ground. In periods of stasis, money circulates through an organization, but without urgency, since its generation and expenditure become as automatic as breathing. Then, at various stages of growth or crisis, capital becomes absolutely essential again—and usually, much less money is flowing in than out. There is no hot and cold running money tap in most corporate head-quarters, as some critics of capitalism seem to believe. Nor do most companies have huge reserves on hand. Money is more like electricity for most businesses: consumed immediately (speed-of-light thing) at the moment of generation.

When Gary began building, he had to amass construction funds and then enough money to keep the hotel afloat until it started producing at least enough revenue to cover debt service, taxes and operational costs. Then he needed to access considerable capital to build more hotels—especially as his building pace more than doubled from 1987 to 1988 (from two to five hotels) and then tripled from 1988 to 1989 (from five to 16 hotels). From 1989 through 1996, Gary's building pace almost tripled again before leveling off at about 30 hotels per year—still a rapid rate compared to private competitors who struggled to build five or more new hotels a year—as the century came to a close, as shown in the graph on the following page.

As indicated previously, access to capital is the largest hurdle for business ventures in the early years. How do businesspeople get going? Gary generated enough financial resources via his insurance business to buy two small hotels and then fund the construction of several small hotels. But how did Gary ramp up his production so dramatically after getting Tharaldson Enterprises to first base? His revenues were not nearly strong enough to cover the construction costs for 16 hotels, let alone repeat that output the next year and keep accelerating.

Recurring recessions were complicating relationships with lenders, the primary gateways to capital. The U.S. Federal Reserve raised interest rates in

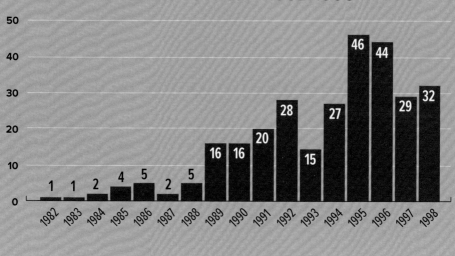

New Hotels Built Per Year   1982-1998

the 1980s to battle stagflation that was causing sluggish economic growth.

The late 1980s and early 1990s also saw the savings and loan (S&L) crisis, during which a third of the nation's 3,234 S&L institutions failed. There were many causes of the crisis, which cost taxpayers $132 billion, but the main effect was significantly higher interest rates on loans at all banks and the dampening of economic growth. Gary borrowed from an S&L to build a Comfort Inn in Lincoln, Nebraska, without experiencing any direct difficulties, but he does recall 14 percent interest rates at the time.

Major banks, as a result, were reluctant to lend to Gary, a new entrepreneur, because of the listless economy and high interest rates, which increased their perception of risk. As well, the conventional wisdom in the hospitality industry at the time was that hotels were overbuilt. This was true regarding full-service hotels and economy and mid-priced brands in major urban areas. In fact, many hotel owners suffered financial difficulties during this decade and sold properties or declared bankruptcy. Hotel developers, in response, were more inclined to buy existing venues and convert them to a desired brand.

Better quality limited-service flags (an industry term for brands), such as Fairfield Inn, and extended-stay hotels, such as Residence Inn, were still in their infancy. The tremendous growth potential that Gary perceived wasn't yet obvious at the corporate offices of big banks in major cities.

"Apparently, Gary never read the memo the rest of us did about how difficult it was to borrow money for new hotel construction in the early '90s," Daryl Nickel, Marriott's Executive Vice President for Corporate Development, said during his award presentation speech at the first Hunter Investment Conference Inaugural Award for Excellence and Inspiration in 2010. "[W]henever he found a site he liked, he went to the local banker and sold him on the viability of the project and the benefits to the community."

The key here is "local." Gary believed that local banks throughout the Midwest would have a different view. To begin, he knew they needed loans to survive since they weren't handling massive union pension funds, for example, which could sustain big-city financial institutions. The challenge was to present local bankers with a convincing story and the data to back up his ask. Local bankers knew their markets and could easily agree that the aging Ramada or no-name motels were outdated.

Since Gary underbuilt his hotels, his breakeven point was 50 percent occupancy. This meant that in normal and good times, his hotels were quite profitable. More importantly from a risk management perspective, this also meant that in economic downturns, Gary's lodgings would show enough profit to cover debt service and survive. This was especially appealing to bankers in the 1980s and early 1990s, when many smaller hospitality companies went out of business in sluggish economies.

Significantly, Gary was able to negotiate lower equity needs for new construction. Construction loans typically required 20 to 25 percent equity. However, since Gary functioned as his own contractor, he pledged the contracting fees towards equity. Gary also held a real estate license, which he used to purchase hotel sites. Usually he split the 6 percent real estate fees with the local agent with whom the property was listed and pledged his half-portion to the bank towards equity. Both pledges enabled him to get construction loans with only 15 percent equity.

The equity required to build 16 hotels in 1989 (eight Comfort Inns, five Days Inns, two Super 8s and one Quality Inn) was $3.5 million, which is 15 percent of the $23.3 million needed to build these hotels (all-in cost).

To cover this need, Gary sold nine hotels for $5 million net (after debt service). This also gave him all of the equity he needed for the 16 hotels he built the following year. In total, Gary sold 13 hotels between 1987 and 1991 and invested all the proceeds into equity for new hotels.

"The local banks understood my strategy of building smaller hotels at a lower price point with the best franchise," Gary explained. "Super 8 was very good when we started and then we moved up to Comfort Inns, which were very strong in the 1980s and early1990s."

However, Gary didn't have enough hotels to sell to sustain the 2,250 percent increase in his building pace from 1987 through 1996. Refinancing existing properties, he found, was the easiest story to sell to banks since it had already happened. In exact detail, he could show lenders the occupancy rates, average daily room rates, revenues and net profits for hotels that were already built and operating. No guesswork was involved, so bankers didn't need to worry about overly optimistic projections of performance. In fact, Gary always made conservative projections, even when trying to convince loan officers to back a project. "Under-promise and over-deliver" was a mantra in all of Gary's dealings, which added to his positive reputation in the financial community.

Refinancing regulations at the time allowed him to apply for a loan based on the hotel's appraised value. This was about 25 percent higher than the building cost. Since the loan was typically for about 80 percent of the appraised value, Gary was able to get back all the cash he had used to build the property. To illustrate, consider construction costs for a Fairfield Inn in the early 1990s:

Construction cost:	$1.96 million (80 rooms)
All-in Cost:	$2.587 million
Appraised Value:	$2.45 million
Loan:	$1.96 million (80 percent of appraised value)

To build a Fairfield Inn circa 1990, the per-room construction cost was $24,500. The total cost, including land, FF&E, fees, licenses and other expenses, was about 32.5 percent higher, equaling about $32,400 per room. The all-in cost is less uniform than the construction cost since land prices,

THARALDSON ENTERPRISES

HOW THARALDSON ENTERPRISES STACKS UP WITHIN THE U.S. AND WITH THE REST OF THE WORLD

RANKINGS WITHIN THE U.S.

TOP TEN BY NUMBER OF HOTELS 2004

RANK	OWNER/COMPANY	NO. OF HOTELS
1	THARALDSON ENTERPRISES	358
2	HOSPITALITY PROPERTIES TRUST	272
3	WESTMONT HOSPITALITY GROUP	209
4	FELCOR LODGING TRUST	161
5	CNL HOTELS & RESORTS	128
6	HOST MARRIOTT CORP.	113
7	MARCUS HOTELS & RESORTS	98
8	LODGIAN INC.	96
9	MERISTART HOSPITALITY CORP.	93
10	EQUITY INNS	93

TOP TEN BY NUMBER OF ROOMS 2004

RANK	OWNER/COMPANY	NO. OF ROOMS
1	HOST MARRIOTT CORP.	56,931
2	FELCOR LODGING TRUST	45,742
3	HOSPITALITY PROPERTIES TRUST	34,284
4	CNL HOTELS & RESORTS	28,842
5	WESTMONT HOSPITALITY GROUP	28,027
6	THARALDSON ENTERPRISES	26,220
7	MERISTART HOSPITALITY CORP.	24,729
8	COLUMBIA SUSSEX CORP.	19,480
9	LODGIAN INC.	18,164
10	JQ HAMMONS HOTELS & RESORTS	15,254

Source: Hotel Business® Research

RANKINGS OF ROOM OWNERSHIP INTERNATIONALLY 2001

RANK	COMPANY	ROOMS	HOTELS
1	CENTANT CORP.	553,771	6,624
2	SIX CONTINENTS HOTELS	511,072	3,274
3	MARRIOTT INTERNATIONAL	435,983	2,398
4	ACCOR	415,774	3,654
5	CHOICE HOTELS INTERNATIONAL	362,549	4,545
6	HILTON HOTELS CORP.	327,487	1,986
7	BEST WESTERN INTERNATIONAL	306,851	4,052
8	STARWOOD HOTELS & RESORTS WORLDWIDE	224,467	743
9	CARLSON HOSPITALITY WORLDWIDE	135,066	788
10	HYATT HOTELS CORP./HYATT INTERNATIONAL	88,442	204
15	WYNDHAM INTERNATIONAL	57,211	224
18	EXTENDED STAY AMERICA	45,452	431
20	U.S. FRANCHISE SYSTEMS	40, 892	500
32	WHITBREAD HOTEL COMPANY	26,572	357
33	MGM MIRAGE	26,375	18
37	WALT DISNEY COMPANY	23,863	21
38	THARALDSON ENTERPRISES	23,788	341*
62	HARRAH'S ENTERTAINMENT	13,500	25
91	WHITE LODGING SERVICES	9,059	73

Source: Hotels Magazine

RANKINGS WORLDWIDE

HOTELS' CORPORATE 300 RANKING INTERNATIONALLY BY THE NUMBER OF ROOMS OWNED
*THARALDSON ENTERPRISES RANKED 17TH IN THE WORLD IN HOTEL PROPERTY OWNERSHIP.

HOSPITALITY INDUSTRY
ILLUSTRATED

EMPLOYMENT IMPACT

4.5 MILLION
JOBS
Direct Impact

8 MILLION
JOBS
Supported by
Operations and Guest Spending

3.5 MILLION
JOBS
Indirect Impact

U.S. LODGING PROPERTIES

33,000
of These
Properties are
Small Businesses

54,200
Lodging
Properties
in the U.S.

5 MILLION
Total
Guest Rooms

1.1 BILLION
Occupied
Room Nights
Annually

ECONOMIC IMPACT

For Every **$100** Spent on lodging → An Additional **$221** Spent in the Community

$245 BILLION
Spent On-Site

$56 BILLION
Food Beverage

$64 BILLION
Recreation/Retail

$118 BILLION
transportation

$238 BILLION
Spent Off-Site Within the Community

$483 BILLION
Total Guest Spending

$167 BILLION
Generated in Federal/State/Local Taxes

$650 BILLION
TOTAL IMPACT OF U.S. HOTEL INDUSTRY

fees and environmental regulations vary significantly from state to state and city to city.

Although Gary was typically building 60- to 70-room Fairfield Inns at the time, the example on page 96 uses 80 rooms so that a comparison can be made with building the same hotel eight years later. Included in the cost analysis are three of the other Marriott flags Gary was building. Please note the different room counts in the prototypes for Residence Inn, TownePlace Suites and Courtyard. From 1990 through 1998, costs increased at 4 percent per year, which accounts for cost increases.

Rick Larson, who took over as chief of hotel development for Gary in the mid-1990s, recalled that Gary's competitors could not believe he built a Residence Inn for about $60,000 per key, while they couldn't get one done for less than $80,000 per room. These are construction, not all-in, costs.

Interestingly, Gary set room rates at $1.50 per thousand dollars (or 1.5 in common parlance) of the all-in key cost. The nightly rate at Residence Inn, therefore, was about $95 per night in the mid-1990s, while at a Fairfield Inn, it was $55.

Also, by the mid-1990s, most of Gary's new hotels had 60-plus rooms, as he targeted urban centers in what he called the "sweet spot" (60,000 to 70,000 residents) and in sweeter spots: larger cities. The bottom line was that Gary kept costs, motel size and brands in sync with the markets he was targeting. He could provide competitive room rates and still make a profit, even in down cycles. This created tremendous appeal among local bankers. Also, Gary could afford to pay his employees well and was not skimping on quality to save money and stay afloat. Win, win, win, win.

———————

Another factor that powered Gary's growing empire was the remarkable fact that "almost all of my properties kicked off with a lot of cash," he said, meaning that within a month of opening, the new hotels were showing a return. Not only were there substantial profit margins because of his operational efficiencies and innovations, prime locations and customer service, but these caused the property to function in the black almost immediately. After debt service and operating expenses, each new hotel built from 1986 to 1990 produced about $80,000 in cash flow per year. In the 1990s, cash flow grew to $100,000 per hotel with 15-year amortization. The 44 hotels that opened in 1996, for example, returned almost $4.5 million per annum by the end of 1997. Profits were reinvested immediately into building new hotels, creating a fiscal trampoline effect—without the downside.

Back in 1985, the revenue from Gary's 10 open hotels was $1.9 million, yielding a net cash flow of $385,000. Gary also had a net cash flow of $220,000 from his insurance company. Six years later, the net cash flow reached $5.3 million, which doubled by 1991, as room sales at all hotels brought in more than $33 million.

By 1997, revenue for Tharaldson Motels, Inc. (TMI), which was formed in 1993 and held 80 percent of Gary's lodging portfolio, rocketed to $200.4 million with $41.3 million in net cash flow. Four years later, TMI took in $269.4 million and yielded $60.6 million in cash flow.

Accordingly, Gary's net worth (assets minus liabilities) grew rapidly from $245,775 in 1980 to $2.9 million when he owned only four hotels. By 1989, Gary's net worth had increased almost sixfold to $17 million. Two years later, this had more than tripled to $49.6 million, when Gary owned 72 hotels and had 28 more under construction. As a result, his net worth took another leap to $65.5 million in 1992. The business community started to take notice and presented Gary with the 1992 North Dakota Business Innovator of the Year Award, presented by the University of North Dakota. The next year he was awarded the Ernst & Young Entrepreneur of the Year in hospitality, as his net worth grew to almost $97 million.

Still, Gary's personal bank accounts were not swelling enormously, precisely because he was reinvesting the profits back into Tharaldson Enterprises in the form of equity for new hotels, as well as for development expenses and bridging operational costs until hotels became profitable. Even though his hotels were typically profitable after a month, he still had to cover operating costs for each property for the first month. Since he averaged 28.5 hotels per year in the 1990s, this amounted to considerable capital.

During his speech at the Hunter award ceremony, Daryl Nickel said, "Every franchisor wanted their brands on the Gary Tharaldson Express." Clearly they were not the only ones. Local banks throughout the Midwest were also boarding the Gary Tharaldson Express. "By the mid-1990s, Gary was dealing with over 100 banks," Nickel said. "If Gary wanted to borrow more than the banker's lending limit, Gary personally recruited other banks to participate. He was also willing to sign personally. Once the banks got to know Gary and saw his operating results, they chased him."

Gary was the first developer in the lodging industry to syndicate loans since his pace of building hotels soon exhausted the capacity of local banks. Instead of going to big banks, Gary spread his borrowing out among many banks—as many as 100 banks simultaneously for up to 46 construction loans, as in 1995. In finance, a group of lenders is referred to as a syndicated bank facility.

Gary learned early that hotel brands matter. Building the best brands for his target markets—both geographic and demographic—gave Gary a competitive advantage. Higher occupancy and room rates translated directly to the bottom line, which enabled Gary to build more and better brands.

In the early 1980s, Gary saw Super 8 as best suited to the budget market in the Midwest. The brand was christened "Super 8" because the original room rate was $8.88. Gary built eight Super 8s in the early 1980s and then averaged less than one per year, building 14 in total. His last Super 8 opened in 1994. Other brands in this sector included Econo Lodge, Sleep Inn, Quality Inn, Days Inn and Americinn, of which Gary built 15 in total from 1985 through 1999.

By 1986, Gary was transitioning to Comfort hotels, which included two variations: Comfort Inn and Comfort Suites. Comfort Suites offers more space and amenities, so the room rates are 15 to 20 percent higher. Gary considered building and running Comfort hotels to be a significant step up in quality from Super 8 and similar brands without being too "spendy." Comfort hotels also included a swimming pool, which Super 8 did not offer at the time. Gary put the pool and corridors inside the Comfort structures.

For a hotel to add "& Suites" to its name—such as Country Inn & Suites or Fairfield Inn & Suites—at least 10 percent of the rooms must be suites. If the hotel's moniker is "Suites," as in SpringHill Suites, then every room is a suite. These come in different configurations—studio, one bedroom and two bedrooms—but always include separate areas to sleep and work. Some have full kitchens and appeal to the extended-stay traveler, while others include a mini-fridge and microwave. When Gary started building "& Suites," he spent about 6 percent more in construction costs to add enough suites to qualify for the classification. The suites added 10 to 12 percent to the hotel's yearly revenue, which is a terrific return on investment.

"Our Comfort hotels kicked ass to begin with," Gary recalled. He built the first two Comfort hotels in 1986 in Lincoln and Omaha, Nebraska, respectively. By the end of 1998, Gary had built a total of 70 Comfort hotels and purchased an additional eight of them.

"The guy who scrimps and saves to own that one hotel and puts in his seven-days-a-week, 14-hour days, that's admirable," said Richard Kaden, Choice's Senior Vice President of Franchise Operations, in an article in Lodging magazine in October 1996, "but that guy is probably doing all he's going to do. What we want are the [Gary] Tharaldsons of the world, people who are going to do multiple properties each year."

Unfortunately for Choice Hotels, Gary was moving away from their brands at the time. This was not because the quality of Choice brands was slipping or because relations with this franchisor were troubled. In fact, Gary still speaks highly of Choice Hotels and is very grateful for the role the brands played in his success. However, "Choice didn't produce another competitive brand to build out, especially at the upper end," he said. When Gary started in 1982, he could construct a Comfort Inn almost anywhere he chose. But by the end of the 1990s, there were few opportunities left and he was entering his most prolific period. Currently, there are 1,678 Comfort hotels (1,113 Comfort Inns and 565 Comfort Suites) in the U.S.

Gary began to transition to the three top franchise companies in 1992: Marriott (now Marriott International, Inc.), Hilton (now Hilton Worldwide Holdings, Inc.) and IHG (now InterContinental Hotels Group, PLC). Marriott and Hilton were and remain Gary's first two choices. If one of their flags is not available in a prospective location, he considers other brands.

Until the end of 1991, Dobmeier, Gary and a few employees at the Fargo headquarters "did everything involved in opening new hotels. We trained the new staff. We got the furniture, bedding, office supplies—everything,"

Dobmeier recounted. "Then we started putting together teams to go out and open hotels," since the pace of opening hotels was both relentless and accelerating.

"Urgency was a word that existed in Gary's vocabulary," Dobmeier recalled. "When he wanted something done, we went and did it."

In 1992, as Gary was approaching 100 hotels, Tharaldson Enterprises had T-shirts made with the slogan "200 by 2000."

"Gary wasn't always easy to work for in my position because we were pushing for results," Dobmeier said. "A little impatient sometimes."

If there were delays Gary judged unnecessary, "he'd come into my office and chew my ass out," recalled Dobmeier. "I'd be sick to my stomach." Ten minutes later, Gary would come back and invite him for lunch.

"I'd say, 'Gary, let me calm down here first and then I'll go to lunch with you,'" Dobmeier related. "He wasn't holding anything personal against me or anyone, but he quickly got his point across of what he expected. I was a competitor too, so we were always on the same wavelength. We didn't want to lose."

For Gary's part, "I can never hold a grudge." Nor were "ass-chewings" a regular event. He tried to find the right balance between giving direction and needed corrections and avoiding over-managing his directors and managers.

"I know every day what's going on, the important metrics. If it's not going right, I want to know why. More importantly, I want to know what is being done to correct it, or if it's not correctable," Gary said. "Sometimes I see a blip in occupancy and call Aimee Fyke, my head of operations. She says, 'A group of 30 people just left. They didn't know the exact date they were going to check out so we couldn't book the rooms.'"

Dobmeier compared Gary to "the one-minute manager" after the book of the same title by Kenneth Blanchard, PhD, and Spencer Johnson, MD, published in 1982, which Gary read. The book articulates three effective management techniques: one-minute goals, one-minute praise and one-minute reprimands.

Gary was also the one-minute decision-maker. "He was the owner, the entrepreneur and the risk-taker," Dobmeier said. "To make decisions, he didn't have to go to a board of trustees. Getting things done was a lot easier because when we had meetings and discussed things, he would make a decision right in front of us. We walked out of there and got on it right away."

In April 1996, Gary opened his 200th hotel. "We blew by that '200 by 2000' by quite a bit," he recalled with brightening eyes.

Only once did Dobmeier push back against Gary. "We were thinking of leaving our health insurance company and I told him this was the wrong decision." Health insurance costs were escalating dramatically and Gary was considering paying employees to find insurance on their own.

"That's who we are and I don't want us to see our people having to deal with it on their own," Dobmeier argued. "It's our responsibility to continue providing health insurance."

Gary considered Dobmeier's position—for a few moments—and then changed his mind. Otherwise, Dobmeier had complete confidence in Gary's decisions. Although Dobmeier was empowered by Gary to make tactical decisions on his own, "I ran a lot of stuff by him just because I wanted him to be aware maybe of what I was doing or thinking. In 1995, we're going to open 46 hotels and then 44 hotels the next year and I would discuss how we're going to do it. We didn't get into arguments because we didn't need to. My job was to figure out how we're going to reach our goals."

Almost everyone works at a company or organization at some point in their careers where much, if not most, of their time and energy is wasted on battling bad decisions from various layers of management. This accounts for many of the failures to reach objectives. At Gary's companies, no time or effort was lost by poor decision-making, which empowered the company's growing success.

Not only Dobmeier, but every employee had confidence in the objectives Gary set and the myriad of tactical decisions along the way. They got on and stayed on the Gary Tharaldson Express.

The Express didn't build itself, even as Gary solved cash flow and bank loan challenges. In the late 1980s and early 1990s, Gary made several important hires including Larry Madson, Aimee Fyke and Rick Larson.

In the late 1970s, Madson worked as a general contractor building houses in Fargo. With high interest rates curtailing the home building industry in the early 1980s, he moved to Denver and worked as a carpenters' superintendent framing apartment buildings.

Needing a job when he returned to Fargo in September 1988, Madson contacted Jamie Johnson, a friend who worked for Gary as a subcontractor. Madson was put to work immediately as a carpenter building the Comfort Suites in South Fargo. "I laid out the entire building—that's cutting all the walls and laying out the studs and headers," he recalled.

After Thanksgiving that year, Madson drove to Moline, Illinois, to start building Gary's Comfort Inn there. He so impressed Don Kauers, Gary's construction manager at the time, with the quality of his work that Gary's brother Roger, who was the construction superintendent for Gary's Comfort Suites, asked him to become a construction superintendent. A year later, in 1989, Gary flew to Danville, Illinois, where Madson had just started working on Gary's Comfort Inn.

"He took me to lunch, which was a burger joint, and offered me an incentive to continue to keep working for him," Madson recounted. "Gary offered partial ownership in the properties that I would be building, which was a very good benefit." Good, indeed, as Madson would learn that small percentages in Gary's hotels eventually turned into millions of dollars.

Soon Madson was the project manager for the Illinois area, doing his job as a happy piston in the locomotive engine of the Gary Tharaldson Express.

"Basically, Gary created the industry of limited-service hotels that didn't exist in smaller towns. Then all the big players started copying him and selling franchises to everybody," Madson said. "He's a remarkable guy, one of those people who sees things and does them before anybody else. You look at it in hindsight and say, 'Oh, yeah, why didn't I think of that?' It was so obvious but nobody else saw it."

What impressed Madson was Gary's faith in him and his generosity. When he returned from Denver and started working for Gary, his finances were shaky after some personal difficulties. Gary cosigned a bank note so Madson could buy a vehicle to get to work—before he knew Madson well.

"If it wasn't for Gary," said Madson, "I don't know where I would've ended up."

Fyke graduated from Southern University of Illinois Carbondale with a bachelor of science degree in hospitality management in 1988 and then worked for a year in management at the 1,200-room Chicago Marriott Downtown Magnificent Mile. Then she transferred to the Chicago Marriott Oakbrook, also a classic premium hotel, in suburban Chicago.

Fyke commuted to work by car from Evanston, Illinois, 30 miles northeast of Oakbrook. After two years of 90-minute car rides, Fyke was growing weary of commuting, and she didn't want to live in or around a big city. In 1991, Fyke's mother sent her an advertisement from the local newspaper about the general manager's position at the Fairfield Inn that Gary was building in Forsyth—where Fyke and her husband grew up—which borders Decatur, 175 miles south of Chicago. Since the Fairfield is a Marriott brand, Fyke went immediately to the HR department at her hotel and asked for a transfer.

The HR officer discouraged her, intimating that it would be beneath anyone with experience at a full-service Marriott to work at a limited-service hotel, even if it was a Marriott. Also, the officer strongly recommended against working for a franchisee.

Fyke applied for the position anyway and was hired. It turned out that having worked for Marriott was key. Since the Forsyth Fairfield, which opened on June 7, 1991, was one of the first built by a franchisee, the Marriott executives in charge of franchising were recommending that Gary hire managers with Marriott management experience.

Fyke worked as the Forsyth general manager for six months.

"She didn't manage that hotel very long," Dobmeier recounted, "because Gary saw she had the talent to take the next step immediately. We made her an area director with a group of new hotels to manage."

Within five years, at 28 years of age, Fyke was serving as a regional vice president overseeing 40 hotels. She then became the Senior Vice President of Operations for Extended Stay (hotels). Dobmeier was the other Senior Vice President for Select Service (hotels).

Because Fyke worked her way up from entry level management, starting at Marriott, she is able to talk to her employees and say, "I've walked in your shoes. I know how hard you work and I can't tell you how much we appreciate what you do." Like Gary, Fyke has always shown appreciation for the people, from cleaning staff to general managers, who make Tharaldson hotels successful. The buildings don't take care of the guests any more than they clean and maintain themselves.

Because Fyke quickly developed extensive experience with Marriott, Hilton and Choice hotels, she was recruited heavily and often. But she stayed with Gary, realizing that working for him was best for her career and her family.

"Gary took a chance on a young girl from Central Illinois and it's been a great ride. I look at him as my boss, my mentor and as a really good friend," Fyke related. "I've had four children working for Gary, and he includes my family in everything. If we're going to go to dinner, he says to bring everybody. He'll text my son before his Friday night high school football game. My son plays quarterback and he'll get a message from Gary: 'Good luck tonight, Ryan.'"

In 1993, Gary hired Richard H. "Rick" Larson to head his development company. Gary and Larson had met a few years earlier because their sons—Matthew Tharaldson and Greg Larson—played hockey together for the Fargo Flyers as they attended middle school. They were also teammates in high school on the Fargo South Bruins. Since Larson was a real estate developer, he and Gary had lots to talk about as they watched their sons play. Their friendship developed, and in 1993, Gary asked Larson to work for him building hotels.

"I was 43 years old at the time," recalled Larson. "Gary said, 'You've got 10 good years left in you, Rick. That's all I need. Can you give me 10 good years?'"

Larson went home and thought about the offer. "That would put me at 53 and maybe I would want to retire then," he said. Soon he called Gary to say, 'Yes, I've got 10 years.' Well, it's 24 years later and we're still working together."

Larson started as the head of land acquisition. Even when Gary had complete confidence in Larson's judgment, Larson still insisted that Gary give the final OK. By 1995, Larson became head of construction and later was promoted to Senior Vice President of Development.

"I had confidence that Gary was choosing good sites, and when Larson came on board, that confidence grew," Dobmeier recalled. "He really knew sites and he knew quality, the quality of our hotels. And that's when we

At a softball tournament in June 1992 in Fargo, Gary met Connie Green who was playing on a women's slow pitch team. Connie was a 27-year-old biology and health teacher and school counselor at Hawley High School in Hawley, Minnesota, which is 30 miles east of Fargo. She also coached volleyball, basketball and track. On April 23, 1993, they were married at Faith Lutheran Church in Fargo. They played together on the Tharaldson Enterprise's co-ed team that year and then won the 1994 North Dakota State Co-Ed Championship.

moved up from our basic Fairfield Inns and started building larger hotels."

Gary was still underbuilding but in larger markets, where he was constructing a 100-room hotel while competitors were building at 125 to 135 rooms.

Gary's business philosophy, said Dobmeier, "is like the McDonalds and Burger King theory of building beside each other." This involved two crucial tactical innovations in the hospitality business: the multi-brand, multi-segment marketing approach and hotel development as a manufacturing process.

In strategic terms, these innovations constitute prime examples of satisfying the second and third elements of Col. Warden's strategic thinking, as outlined in Chapter Five. To recall, the first element is the Future Picture, or strategic objective. Throughout the 1980s and 1990s, Gary moved his goals up to higher and higher numbers of hotels, as he thought "like an architect—not like a bricklayer," as Warden puts it. Following his 25/40 rule, Gary made a discipline of spending most of his time figuring out how to meet and surpass his objectives.

The second and third elements of strategic thinking are Target Selection and Campaign Timeframe. Gary's primary targets were, and remain, (i) hotel sites (according to the criteria outlined in Chapter Six, with the size of target urban areas increasing gradually); (ii) profitability via innovations, efficiencies and quality control; and (iii) banks, in order to gain access to the capital needed to accelerate the hotel construction pace.

Integral to target selection and the campaign timeframe is the concept Warden coins as "Go to Rome" in the "Concept Summaries" of his course material:

> Almost everyone has a tendency to concentrate on the immediate problem without keeping in mind the real objective. Hannibal won the battle of Cannae through brilliant tactics but failed to follow up by going to Rome. The eventual result was the utter destruction of his civilization. Rome may be a place, but more often it is a state of being. Bill Gates did an excellent job in this area where almost from the beginning, his Rome state of being was a company that had the dominant graphical user interface software and associated applications that were of interest to the majority of computer users."

For Gary, Rome was the place of dominance in the markets he focused on—first, the economy lodging market with Comfort Inn hotels in small- to medium-sized urban centers along interstate highways in the Midwest. By 1994, Gary was building in large cities—such as Corpus Christi, Texas, which had about 265,000 residents in the mid-1990s—and still on major routes.

Gary and Connie on their honeymoon at a Marriott resort on Maui in Hawaii.

In this case, the hotel is located on the major highway running through the city, connecting to the interstate, and beside major shopping malls. At the same time, Gary was building in small- to mid-sized cities, such as Rochester, Minnesota, where Gary opened a Country Inn & Suites on the same day as his Residence Inn opened in Corpus Christi. There were still solid opportunities in minor urban centers.

If he had tried to enter markets the size of Corpus Christi any earlier, "I might have fallen flat on my face," Gary said. He first needed, he admitted, to master the hotel business and mature as a leader. "I just kept moving up the

Three hotels, a Hampton Inn, a Farifield Inn, and a Residence Inn, that Gary built next to each other in Corpus Christi, TX, in 1995.

ladder to what we are today."

Coincidentally, the mile markers on these and all other highways in the U.S. were laid out in imitation of mile markers on Roman highways through the ancient empire, which marked the distances to Rome—since all roads literally led to Rome.

Although axiomatic now, when Gary initiated the multi-brand/multi-segment approach, no one had ever thought of it in the hotel business. As today, it was normal to see several hotels in the same area, just as the classic Restaurant Row is *de rigeur* in most cities.

"I did this from a business standpoint," Gary explained. "I felt that sometimes when I found a site for a Fairfield Inn, there was room for a Residence Inn right beside it and maybe a Courtyard Inn, too."

In 1995, in Corpus Christi, Texas, Gary built three hotels right next to each other, as shown in the photo above. Since then, the Hampton Inn was converted to a Country Inn & Suites.

As an article in Forbes Magazine in 1997 detailed: "Where possible, Tharaldson builds three or four hotels at the same intersection to improve his chances of snagging a customer. Barrel down Interstate 29 in Fargo, N.D. and you'll see the red brick Econo Lodge, where you can stay for $28. Next door is a Comfort Inn, where the extra $13 a night gets you a Jacuzzi and an indoor pool. At the adjacent Comfort Suites, $48 buys a room with a fridge and microwave. Tharaldson owns all three."

The best example of Gary's multi-brand/multi-segment tactic occurred in Las Vegas, where he built four hotels next to each other at the same time. "They thought I was crazy," Gary recalled with a broad smile—as he should. The hotels—Fairfield Inn, Holiday Inn Express, Residence Inn and Courtyard Inn—performed well. The hotels opened between December 24, 2003 and August 16, 2004. On a typical night at present, the room rates at this cluster offer a range to suit customer needs: $87 at Fairfield, $111 at Holiday Inn, $134 at Courtyard and $135 at Residence Inn. Not only do these four hotels segment according to price but also according to amenities and purpose. Overnight travelers might pick the Fairfield or pay a bit more for a Holiday Inn Express or Hampton Inn, which are a step up in quality. Business travelers, Gary said, often prefer Courtyard, and business and personal travelers, especially families, will likely choose Residence Inn, Homewood Suites or SpringHill Suites for an extended stay.

In 2017, the location for the new stadium for the Las Vegas Raiders NFL football team, which will be built for the 2020 season, was announced: directly across Russel Road, as shown in the map on page 236. A fifth hotel, facing the new stadium site, is a Staybridge Suites, which Gary opened in 2008. Gary definitely has the gift of site sense, if not entirely the sixth sense. He sold the first four hotels in 2006 as part of a package deal because he was offered a higher price for 140 hotels than he thought possible.

Multi-brand/multi-segment complemented Gary's underbuilding tactic—actually put it on steroids. Since his occupancy rates were higher, his hotels often had to turn customers away—well, not quite. With two to four underbuilt hotels in a cluster, it was not unusual for a client to call or walk in and not be able to book a room. However, the manager or desk clerk would immediately place the guest in one of Gary's other nearby hotels. In fact, Gary developed an internal cross-brand sales network, Tharaldson Motel System, which helped his hotels sell 4 to 5 percent more rooms per week elsewhere in the system. This in turn helped boost the average occupancy for all of Gary's hotels to 75 and even 80 percent, which, as Gary remarked, "is very profitable," since every dollar above the breakeven point is mostly pure profit (except for franchise fees).

Instead of allowing competitors to build nearby and take business away, Gary literally cornered the market and became his own competitor. The rival brands he built competed with each other for the highest guest satisfaction, occupancy and profits. Gary rewarded his managers accordingly and rewarded them for referring clients to their rivals within the Tharaldson Motel System.

In the brand area, going to Rome meant building the best—that is, Marriot, Hilton and IHG hotels. From 1990 through 1999, Gary built 158 Marriott hotels, 41 Hiltons and 7 IHGs.

"I say this with the highest degree of respect and admiration," said Bruce White. "Gary was way ahead of the industry and all these Ivy League MBAs in understanding how he could execute a multi-brand, multi-market strategy. He calls it a laboratory out there, where he could figure out what he wanted to do. Gary has received credit in the industry, but not enough for this strategy."

The third component of Col. Warden's strategic thinking is the tactical campaign timeline. This is vitally important for strategic success but is often overlooked. There are two fundamental methods regarding campaign timeframe: either a serial or a parallel attack. A serial attack is sequential, or one step at a time, which usually fails since a serial campaign allows the targeted system to resist and react. For example, if Gary built a Fairfield Inn at a prime intersection but chose not to buy and build on the other one or two or three available sites, then a competitor could easily take advantage. In fact, the presence of Gary's hotel would help the competitor's flag by attracting customers to a quality establishment where they would see the competitor's hotel(s). A Hampton Inn across the street would compete directly with

At the McQuade tournament in 2001, Gary won the 50+ championship, Connie won the top women's championship and Matthew won the top men's championship.

Gary's Fairfield. A Residence Inn next door would cover the extended-stay market and complement the Fairfield—but only if Gary owned both.

In short, by adding a new hotel every 11.8 days, or 31 per year, Gary was blitzing the marketplace—which surrendered. He was not constructing a few hotels at a time, conservatively wading into the lodging industry. Instead, Gary built as many as 46 hotels at the same time in 10 states, as in 1995— that is, as many hotels in prime locations as possible simultaneously to deny competitors and secure the advantage, which included 31 new sources of profit within a month of opening on average.

At this point, he was opening one new hotel every eight days, which seemed a crazed pace, but there was obvious method to the madness. Once Gary demonstrated how to succeed by building smaller versions of well-known brands, he became vulnerable to being copied and losing opportunities. Remarkably, as the reader will see in the next chapter, he helped his competitors as much as he could in terms of information and encouragement. He shared exactly how he made his hotels profitable via his innovations and efficiencies, as well as his hotel site criteria.

Gary trusted his ability to execute and also the prolific speed with which he identified sites and opened hotels. "Incredibly," said Nickel in the Hunter award address, "Gary in 1992 single-handedly accounted for 13 percent of all hotel chain openings in the United States."

At the beginning of his campaign in 1989, Gary was operating 27 hotels (36 built and nine sold) in 10 states. By the end of the decade, Gary ran 296 hotels (18 flags in nine franchising brands) in 29 states. In total, he had built 293 hotels, bought 18 and sold 15 of them.

"It was extraordinary how he could manage the risk of the development game, which most other developers couldn't—certainly at this scale," White said. "Amazingly, Gary would always tell me what his number was five years in advance. He would determine his capital needs and project out how quickly his properties would ramp. He was extraordinary at managing his risk."

Managing risk highlights an essential business paradox. If Gary didn't take risks—that is, if he didn't open so many hotels in such a compressed timeframe—he would have incurred much greater risk of failing to meet his strategic objective of market supremacy.

As novelist Henry Miller wrote (without a single expletive): "One's destination is never a place, but a new way of seeing things." Gary's vision of his destination—destiny, in short—occurred early in his life and guided his business ventures.

The Gary Tharaldson Express was powered by simplicity, which turned Tharaldson Enterprises into a factory. As mentioned earlier, one of Gary's prime mantras was "Keep it simple." In order to build so many hotels so quickly, Gary had to make Tharaldson Enterprises a vertically integrated manufacturing company. It certainly helped that Gary's mind had the simplicity of a computer. He kept the essential development and operational numbers in his head, which he could recall at will and use to make instant calculations.

"Gary thought of himself as a manufacturer, as opposed to what most hotel people consider themselves to be," White said. "They would develop hotels project-by-project as single events."

White talked about how he started in the hotel business by working for Hyatt. "I was always intrigued with running large hotels and being a hotelier in the traditional sense," he said. "Where we differ from Gary is in also developing large, full-service hotels, including thousand-plus-room convention hotels. But Gary stuck to his knitting and stayed in the select-service and extended-stay space."

In accordance with his down-to-earth personality, Gary never felt any fascination with New York City's Ritz-Carlton Central Park or the St. Regis and certainly not the Mandarin Oriental, where the cheapest room currently costs $995 per night. Nor did he ever entertain building a monstrosity such as the 7,000-room Venetian and Palazzo Resort, Hotel & Casino in Las Vegas, which boasts 100,000 square feet of meeting and convention space. And he certainly never had any inclination to deal with a famous chef and his culinary creations, such as Wolfgang Puck and his restaurant at the Hotel Bel-Air in Los Angeles.

In contrast, "we wandered out and did much higher-risk projects, which have been fun, and I'm really glad we did them," White recounted. "Fortunately we've done well with them. But from an academic viewpoint, I could make an argument that Gary's model, from an economic viewpoint and wealth-building viewpoint, is probably a better model than ours."

Gary's independence made simplicity possible. "I had no partners, and there's a great advantage in that," he concluded. "I didn't get slowed down by anybody. As a result, my manufacturing process worked like a charm."

"Gary organized his resources to support his development objectives in a very sequenced way that allowed a very lean organization to be very efficient and effective," White observed. "He has it down so tight that if he invests so much and gets a place built, he's turning a profit within a very short period of time." Almost immediately, Gary was paying off the loan, "so there is minimal risk on an individual property."

"This paid big dividends," White remarked with clear admiration, "and that's why he was able to grow exponentially faster than anybody else. Like many entrepreneurs, he wasn't driven by wanting to accumulate a lot of liquid cash or cash equivalents. He was trying to build something."

"You always set goals," Gary said. "But money is just a means and a measuring stick. It doesn't mean that much to me personally. The game is what I like."

Winning, in Gary's case, neither was, nor is, a compulsion reducible to a psychological imbalance. In fact, the reader will see that Gary has led a very balanced life. Playing "the game" and winning are Gary's vocation, what he is called to do in life—which enables him to positively affect the lives of his employees and the well-being of his various local, regional and national communities.

Gary in his office in Fargo, ND, playing Marriott International Monopoly, 90th Anniversary Edition.

COLLECT $100 SALARY AS YOU PASS GO

CHAPTER EIGHT

Culture, Community & Character

All men's gains are
the fruit of venturing.

Herodotus

Morale is faith in
the man at the top.

Albert S. Johnstone

IN THE LATE 1980s, word about Gary's success was spreading quickly through the hospitality industry and the press. Corporate leaders at Marriott took notice, and Daryl Nickel, the Executive Vice President for Corporate Development, called Gary early in 1989 to recruit him as a franchisee.

"Initially, he was a little reluctant to even talk to us," Nickel recalled. "Gary is very straightforward and just came out and said, 'I understand that people at Marriott are very inflexible, bureaucratic and difficult to deal with.' I answered that we were working hard to change our ways, and we'd love to meet and see if we can do business together."

That year, Gary built eight Comfort Inns and had 20 more in the construction pipeline. From beginning to end, it took Gary about nine months to a year to build a hotel once a site was secured. He was happy with Comfort but intrigued by Marriott, which was regarded as the top hotel company.

Gary agreed to meet and set the date for late April 1989 at his newly opened Days Inn hotel in Davenport, Iowa. Nickel arrived with Todd Clist, Marriott's President of North American Lodging Operations. At lunch, Nickel recalled watching Gary sketch on the back of a paper napkin how he would lay out his first Fairfield Inn.

At the end of their discussion, Gary said, "Alright, let me try a few."

J. Willard Marriott opened the first Marriott hotel in Arlington, Virginia, across the Potomac River from the nation's capital, in 1957. The second hotel opened in a nearby neighborhood two years later. Marriott's son J. Willard "Bill" Marriott, Jr., became president in 1964 and then CEO in 1972, leading the company through five decades of remarkable growth.

From 1957 into the 1980s, the focus of Marriott Corporation was building full-service upscale and luxury hotels. "We had a great model for recycling our capital," said Liam Brown, Marriott's President of Franchising, Owner Services and MxM (Managed by Marriott). "We built hotels and sold them in groups to institutional investors, like pension funds and private equity guys."

The vulnerability of this business model surfaced dramatically in the late 1980s and early 1990s as the economy slowed down and dipped into reces-

The first Fairfield Inn Gary built is in Muncie, IN. It is also the first Fairfield Inn built by a franchisee.

sion. At the same time, tensions grew in the Middle East that led to the Gulf War I, which started in January 1991. REITs (a Real Estate Investment Trust company that owns or finances income-producing real estate such as hotels) and other private and institutional investors sensed trouble in the economy. They stopped buying hotels, especially Marriott properties, since the company had over $3 billion in long-term debt on its balance sheets. Building large, upscale hotels is very capital-intensive and incurs heavy debt loads. After decades of flourishing, Marriott was suddenly in dire financial straits with a serious cash-flow problem.

In response, Marriott looked for growth opportunities in new areas. The company had dabbled in franchising full-service hotels in the late 1960s and early 1970s, which proved unsuccessful because, "[a]s an organization, we simply didn't embrace franchising as wholeheartedly as we needed to make it a success," Bill Marriott wrote in his book, *The Spirit to Serve: Marriott's Way*, which was published by HarperBusiness in 1997.

But as Bill Marriott and other top Marriott officials couldn't help but see, the building of a nationwide interstate highway system had precipitated a growth in economy and mid-priced hotels. In 1981, Marriott decided officially to move beyond hospitality's upscale tier. The first result of that strategic decision was the opening of Courtyard by Marriott in Atlanta, Georgia, in 1983. Courtyard was designed to compete in the moderately priced, business-traveler market.

"By adding 'by Marriott' to the Courtyard brand, the organization crossed a philosophical line," wrote Bill Marriott in his book. "We demonstrated a willingness to throw the weight of the organization behind an innovation that promised—one way or the other, for good or ill—to redefine the core of Marriott. In doing so, we held our breath."

Change is never easy and always presents a challenging paradox: "To grow successfully, you must stay true to who you are, even while working feverishly to change who you are," Marriott wrote.

The Marriott company didn't have to hold its breath for long. Courtyard was a hit, which inspired Marriott to enter the limited-service (also referred to as select-service) hotel arena by opening its first Fairfield Inn in 1987. The new brand, ironically, was named after Fairfield Farm, which J.W. Marriott bought in 1951 for his young family's enjoyment because the property reminded him of the ranches he remembered from growing up in rural Utah. The property is located in the foothills of Virginia's Blue Ridge Mountains and was once owned by the King of England—not exactly an economy-minded guest.

Fairfield was designed in the late 1980s to compete in the limited-service lodging sector against brands such as Comfort Inn, Days Inn and Hampton Inn, which dominated the "under $45 per night" market at the time. The first location, built by Marriott, opened in Atlanta in October 1987. The hotels were configured to appeal to business travelers and families needing fewer amenities—such as no full-service restaurant and the standardization of architecture, bedding and so on—which cut construction and operational costs. Fairfields were marketed as "everything you need to propel your productivity." Rooms have working spaces that now include free Wi-Fi, an ergonomic desk and chair, and a business center with printers. These amenities have since become standard across select-service hotels.

Gary opened his first Fairfield Inn in Muncie, Indiana, on June 1, 1990. This was the first Fairfield built by a franchisee. Gary's friend and competitor Bruce White opened his first Fairfield in September 1990 for a close second.

The Muncie site is strategically located near the intersection of two major roads on the city's outskirts, which had 71,035 residents according to the 1990 census. Nearby is the city's main suburban shopping area, as well as Ball State University, with 22,000 students, and a major art museum.

Then on November 30, Gary opened his second Fairfield in Anderson, Indiana (60,000 residents in 1990), near the intersection of a state and an interstate highway, which funnels into Indianapolis less than 40 miles away. The neighborhood is suburban and near a shopping mall, big box stores and restaurants.

As Nickel said in presenting Gary with the Hunter Conference award in 2010, the "innovations and efficiencies" Gary brought to the hotel industry are "legendary." When Nickel first met Gary in 1989, "we were corporately building Fairfield Inns at Marriott with 135 or more rooms, vinyl siding, exterior corridors, a small outdoor pool. Even with that high room count, these ugly ducklings were costing us over $40,000 per room. Gary showed us how to build attractive, interior-corridor Fairfield Inns with as few as 60 rooms, sized to fit the market, and an inviting indoor pool and a very inviting price tag of less than $25,000 per room." As noted in the previous chapter, this was the per-room construction cost at the time, not the all-in cost.

Before building even his first Fairfield, Gary redesigned the model to put the exterior corridors and the pool inside the structure, as he had done with previous brands. This was a major step forward for Fairfield, one that elevated the look of the establishment and saved significantly on heating and cooling costs. Gary served on the Fairfield Inn advisory board, and many of the innovations he developed in Choice and Super 8 hotels became standards for Fairfield.

In 1991, Marriott hosted a meeting to map out the company's franchising future with only a few attendees, whom Marriott considered the top franchisees. These included: Gary; White; Tom Walsh, founder and CEO of Ocean Properties Hotels Resorts & Affiliates; Phil Ruffin, a highly successful

On February 4, 1997, Gary was presented with Marriott's Partnership Circle Award by Marriott executives, including (left to right) Jerry O'Neill, Daryl Nickel, Mike Collins and Todd Clist. Gary is second from the right.

businessman who owns casinos, hotels and other interests; John Ferguson, president and founder of Ferguson Hotel Group; and B. Gene Carter, founder and Chairman of Texas Western Hospitality.

The meeting was held at the Griffin Gate Marriott Resort & Spa on the outskirts of Lexington, Kentucky. Somewhat ironic was the fact that this upscale Marriott was everything that Gary's hotels weren't: luxurious with an award-winning restaurant and a golf course designed by famed architect Rees Jones, who won the top award from golf course superintendents in 2004. Luxury, of course, comes with a high price, and it wasn't Gary's company that was in financial trouble.

The Marriott executives told the handful of select attendees that the company intended to restrict the number of franchisees to those in the room. They miscalculated only by 900 franchisees and counting, with Gary playing a major role in the growth of Marriott's franchise brands and in attracting hundreds of high-quality franchisees.

By the time Gary opened his third Fairfield Inn in Forsyth, Illinois, in June 1992, he saw that "the numbers just blew us away." Gary knew Marriott was a reputable hotel company, but "at first, I didn't understand how strong

Marriott was. By being the Marriott in town, we were the top choice. There was always another competing hotel brand that was close. Holiday Inn was really good, but we got more than our share of business."

Occupancy rates at Gary's Fairfields ran about 80 percent on average soon after opening, which is astounding considering that on Sundays and holidays the rate is typically around 50 percent. Also, "the Marriott name alone commanded an automatic ten-dollar price tag," Gary recalled. That amounted to a 20 percent room-rate increase at the time. And the Marriott advantage persisted, since Marriott "kept their properties up really well," he noted.

As Nickel remarked, with admiration and perhaps some good-natured envy—both of which were shared by all participants at the award ceremony—"Gary's Fairfield Inns also achieved a much higher ADR than ours."

ADR, which stands for average daily rate, is a common financial metric used to measure performance in comparison to similar hotels, especially in the same geographic area and business sector. To calculate ADR, divide the room revenue by the number of rooms sold:

$$ADR = \frac{Room\ Revenue}{Rooms\ Sold}$$

If a hotel's daily revenue for rooms is $10,000 and the total number of rooms is 100, then the ADR equals 100. The hotel manager, as well as the owner(s), would compare the hotel's ADR against competitors. Let's say there are two hotels nearby competing in the same market vis-à-vis price, service and amenities. One hotel took in the same $10,000 that day, but it's a larger venue with 120 rooms. The ADR would, therefore, be lower at $83.33. Then the second competing hotel also took in the same amount. However, since this lodging has only 80 rooms, the ADR increases to $125.

What this indicates is that the smallest hotel in this group is the most profitable, since building costs, debt service and operating costs (including compensation) are significantly lower. This is exactly what Gary perceived and he configured his business model accordingly. If the ADR for 100-room hotels was 100 in an area, then Gary knew to build smaller, say 60 or 70 rooms. If the ADR for the same hotels was higher, then Gary would build a larger hotel(s). How large would depend on the ADR of 120- and 140-room hotels.

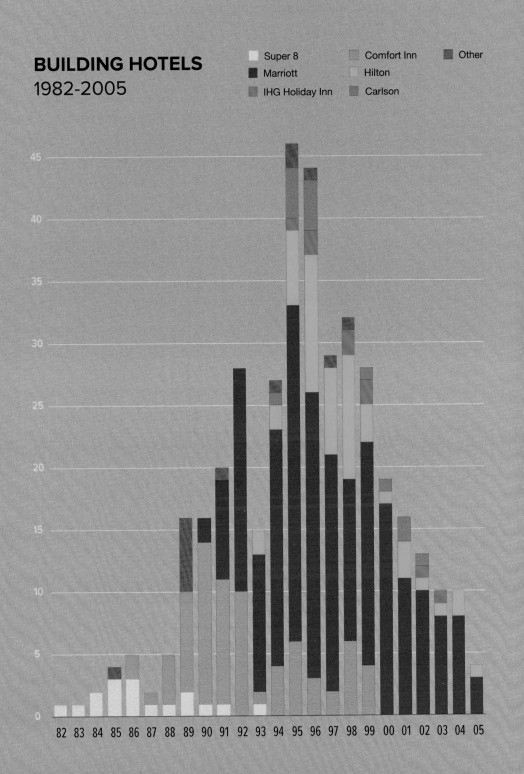

BUILDING HOTELS
1982-2005

Super 8 · Comfort Inn · Other
Marriott · Hilton
IHG Holiday Inn · Carlson

"We never thought that the economics of a 60- to 80-room hotel would ever work," Brown said in his distinct Irish accent. "We thought that the sweet spot was 140 rooms. But Gary showed us how to build, staff and manage a hotel very efficiently and still deliver a great customer experience in a very good box."

Building smaller opened secondary and tertiary markets for Marriott brands—exactly where Gary was building, and there were a lot of those markets.

"Marriott watched us," Gary recalled, "and they saw that we could make more money on a 64-unit than they could on a 135-unit hotel."

One of the biggest advantages of underbuilding is that "you can drive room rates up because you're full," Gary explained. This increases the hotel's ADR, which indicates better profitability.

Also, lower costs and higher occupancy and room rates brought the breakeven point down to 50 percent occupancy or even lower. In contrast, larger hotels had to do better than that by 10 percent or more, which is difficult given that hotels tend to empty out on weekends and holidays.

This was one of the major reasons Gary was able to keep building through recessions in the 1980s and 1990s. Banks understood the fundamentals of his strategic campaign. Not only did the right location and underbuilding guarantee returns even in economic downturns, but the risk was greatly reduced by the simple fact that a much smaller loan was needed to get the project built and operating at a profit. Other franchisees and franchisors marveled at Gary's meteoric rise that kept on streaking across the hospitality skies.

After building two Fairfields in 1990, Gary quadrupled the production of Fairfields to eight the next year. Then he more than doubled it again to 17 Fairfields in 1992, the same year that he began experimenting with other Marriott flags that the company wanted to franchise. First and foremost was Residence Inn, Marriott's premier entry into the extended-stay market.

On November 24, 1992, Gary opened his first Residence Inn in Appleton, Wisconsin. Again, the choice of location was superb. The hotel was built in a city with 66,000 residents at the time and near a major interchange on the interstate connecting Green Bay and Milwaukee. The Appleton Residence Inn

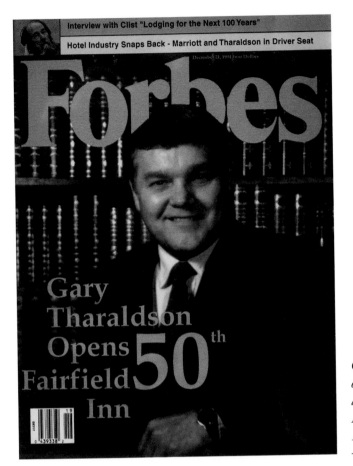

Interview with Clist "Lodging for the Next 100 Years"

Hotel Industry Snaps Back - Marriott and Tharaldson in Driver Seat

December 21, 1994 Four Dollars

Forbes

Gary Tharaldson Opens 50th Fairfield Inn

Gary was featured on the cover and in an article in Forbes Magazine on December 21, 1994.

is located near the Fox River Mall, which opened in 1984 and is currently the state's second-largest mall, with more than 180 stores and restaurants.

There is no restaurant, nor are banquet or convention services offered at Residence Inn hotels. The brand, however, offers an extensive array of amenities, including a business center, small meeting rooms, fitness room, guest laundry facility, market pantry, grocery shopping service, indoor and/or outdoor pool and whirlpool, and valet dry cleaning.

As an upscale, extended-stay hotel, Residence Inn suites come in well-appointed studio, one- and two-bedroom configurations with ample work space, including a desk and free Wi-Fi access, as well as a full kitchen and separate living and dining areas. The brand's slogan—"It's not a room. It's a Residence"—is quite appropriate.

The hotel's market segment includes business travelers and middle-class-to-affluent families who are visiting for an extended period or who simply prefer an apartment environment to a hotel room. The availability of a full kitchen might appeal to a family even for a night or two.

Residence Inn's design benefited greatly from Gary's input. Originally, the property included a "Gatehouse"—housing the front desk, common area for meal service, laundry services, swimming pool and exercise room—and several detached buildings with the residences, similar to a condo complex. All the corridors to first-floor suites and passageways between buildings were outside.

Gary redesigned the brand's layout by consolidating the discrete structures into the traditional layout with all suites and the Gatehouse in one building. He also put all the ground-floor corridors and the swimming pool inside the structure—without losing the brand's residential look.

Gary's Residence Inn in Appleton was the brand's first redesigned layout with interior corridors. "We were all thinking, 'Oh, this will never work from the guest's perspective,'" Brown recalled with a laugh.

Gary's layout also made the brand economically feasible in the long term. Originally, "you needed two to three acres per location for the individual pods," Nickel related. Gary's design reduced that by one-third. The original design involved several individual pods such that three acres were required for 96 suites. Gary's redesign used one acre for 60 suites, which cut land needs almost in half and greatly increased operating efficiencies. Otherwise, according to Brown, it would have been impossible to grow the franchise to 755 properties today "because land costs alone would be prohibitively expensive."

From a guest satisfaction perspective, Residence Inn consistently posts among the highest of all the Marriott brands, and "it does very, very well financially," Gary attested. Not only are room rates significantly higher than Fairfield and its competing brands, but Gary's Residence Inns usually beat other extended-stay hotels.

"Gary was always very good for giving us feedback on how well things were going, where there were opportunities for improvement and where we were delivering something too expensively," Brown said. "He pushed us hard to test everything thoroughly to make sure that it worked. 'Success is never final' is our mantra as well as Gary's."

Center of attention

Comfort chain uses Tharaldson in ad campaign

By Jonathan Knutson
STAFF WRITER

Fargo businessman Gary Tharaldson isn't one to brag about his success, but others are.

He recently served as the poster boy — a wealthy, successful one — for a national advertising campaign by Choice Hotels International, parent of the Comfort hotel chain.

A photograph of Tharaldson and a summary of his success with the Comfort chain were used in an advertisement that appeared in recent editions of three trade publications.

Here's part of the ad:

"Gary Tharaldson is a motel-building machine. He opens a new property every 12 days. He's built 70 new properties in the past three years alone. And he's parlayed this furious pace into a personal net worth of some $50 million.

"It's no coincidence that of Gary's 94 properties, 56 of them bear the Comfort sign."

The ad even calls Tharaldson "the most successful hotelier in America."

Now that the ad has appeared, Tharaldson seems embarrassed by that high-flown praise. He says he participated to help Choice Hotels, not to draw attention to himself.

"I'm their largest franchisee and I just viewed it as advertising for them."

He says his personal net worth already was known in the industry, so he had no qualms about including it in the ad.

Tharaldson is owner/president/founder of Tharaldson Enterprises, which was born when he bought a motel in Valley City, N.D., in 1982. The company grew steadily and moved to Fargo in September 1989.

Tharaldson Enterprises currently has its headquarters at 1020 36th St. S.W., Fargo, and is rapidly outgrowing the building. To increase office space, the firm — which will retain its existing headquarters — expects to take over the present Lutheran Health Systems building at 1202 Westrac Drive S.W., Fargo, in the spring of 1994.

Lutheran Health Systems plans to build a 70,000-square-foot office building at 17th Avenue Southwest and 44th Street in Fargo.

This pose of Gary Tharaldson is the centerpiece of Comfort Inn's advertising campaign.

Gary was featured in an ad campaign for Comfort hotels in 1994.

As with Fairfield Inns, Marriott rolled out Residence Inn and TownePlace Suites without offering breakfast. As with Fairfield, Gary insisted on offering breakfast. "He always wanted the right standards to take care of the customer," Brown said. "He was good at pushing the envelope."

Gary made such a positive and powerful impression on Marriott executives that Bill Marriott attended the opening of the Residence Inn in Appleton, Wisconsin, on November 24, 1992. As Brown related, "Mr. Marriott" was looking "to recruit talented franchisees who understood the business really well and had the ability to grow and understand what Marriott is trying to accomplish. The growing partnership with Gary epitomizes that philosophy."

Five years later, Dobmeier accompanied Gary to Roseville, California, where Bill Marriott presented him with an award for building his 100th Fairfield Inn, which opened in Houston on November 24, 1997. Gary was presented with a bottle of Dom Perignon, which he gave to Dobmeier since he seldom drinks. The bottle sat in Dobmeier's office until he retired in 2016.

"Holy smokes, we were getting to be a big company," Dobmeier recalled saying at the time with a smile. By the end of 1999, Gary had built 118 Fairfield Inns and 22 Residence Inns.

He also began building three additional Marriott brands, and by the dawn of the new century, had opened eight Courtyard Inns, six TownePlace Suites and four SpringHill Suites. Marriott hotels accounted for 50 percent of the hotels Gary built through 1999, making him Marriott's largest single franchisee.

Like Residence Inn, SpringHill and TownePlace are all-suite hotels that appeal to families and extended-stay guests. Smith Travel Research rates TownePlace Suites in the Upper Midscale market segment, and SpringHill Suites and Residence Inn in the Upscale Hotel market segment. In 2016, Parents magazine ranked SpringHill Suites third and Residence Inn first in the budget category for traveling families. Although upscale, these two brands prove economical for entire families.

"To Marriott's credit," said White, "they were smart enough to realize quickly that Gary's humble demeanor did not detract from his genius as a developer."

"What really impressed us right away at Marriott," said Brown, "was that you could ask Gary a question about any aspect of operations and he could

RESIDENCE INN COSTS

COMPARATIVE COSTS OVER AN 18 YEAR SPAN

	2018	1998
OPENING YEAR	2018	1998
ROOM COUNT	112	120
Average Room Rate	$120	$90

SECTION	TITLE	RESIDENCE INN PROTOTYPE AVERAGE COST PER ROOM	RESIDENCE INN PROTOTYPE AVERAGE COST PER ROOM	PERCENT INCREASE IN AVERAGE COST PER ROOM
1	CONCRETE & MASONRY	$7,356	$3,065	140%
2	METALS, WOODS & PLASTICS	$17,228	$8,790	96%
3	THERMAL & MOISTURE PROTECTION	$7,345	$2,330	238%
4	DOORS & WINDOWS	$5,467	$2,975	97%
5	FINISHES	$15,418	$4,210	292%
6	SPECIALTIES & SPECIAL CONSTRUCTION	$2,001	$1,700	18%
7	EQUIPMENT	$3,427	$1,890	94%
8	FURNISHINGS	$14,218	$9,760	56%
9	MECHANICAL & CONVEYING SYSTEMS	$26,072	$11,095	135%
10	ELECTRICAL	$11,079	$7,440	60%
SUB-TOTAL BUILDING ONLY		**$109,613**	**$53,255**	**113%**
11	SITEWORK	$7,610	$4,000	104%
SUB-TOTAL BUILDING & SITEWORK ONLY		**$117,223**	**$57,255**	**113%**
12	GENERAL CONDITIONS & FEES*	$12,116	$4,822	151%
PROJECT CONSTRUCTION TOTAL		**$129,339**	**$62,047**	**116%**
	LAND (+12%)	$16,047	$7,446	
	SOFT COSTS (+8%)*	$10,716	$4,964	
	CONTINGENCY COSTS & OVERRUNS (+5%)	$6,467	$3,102	
ALL-IN COST PER ROOM		**$167,412**	**$77,559**	**116%**

*SOFT COSTS:
    ARCHITECTURE & ENGINEERING
    FINANCING COSTS
    FRANCHISE FEES, LEGAL COSTS, PERMITS & FEES
    DEVELOPMENT COSTS

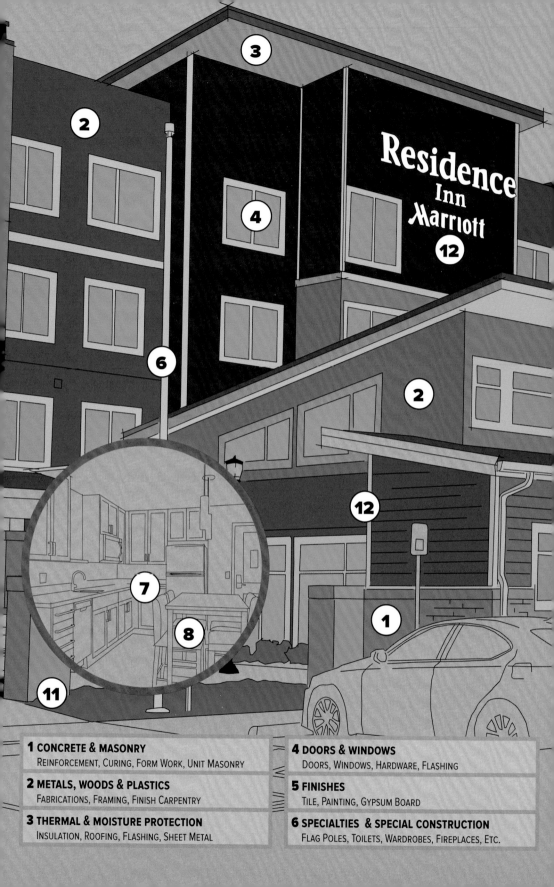

1 CONCRETE & MASONRY
REINFORCEMENT, CURING, FORM WORK, UNIT MASONRY

2 METALS, WOODS & PLASTICS
FABRICATIONS, FRAMING, FINISH CARPENTRY

3 THERMAL & MOISTURE PROTECTION
INSULATION, ROOFING, FLASHING, SHEET METAL

4 DOORS & WINDOWS
DOORS, WINDOWS, HARDWARE, FLASHING

5 FINISHES
TILE, PAINTING, GYPSUM BOARD

6 SPECIALTIES & SPECIAL CONSTRUCTION
FLAG POLES, TOILETS, WARDROBES, FIREPLACES, ETC.

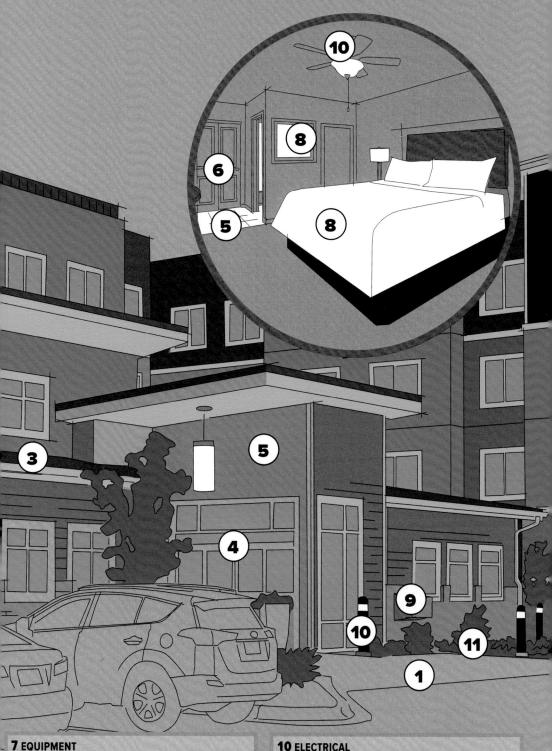

7 EQUIPMENT
LAUNDRY, FOOD SERVICE

8 FURNISHINGS
BEDS, FURNITURE, DECORATIVE

9 MECHANICAL & CONVEYING SYSTEMS
DUCTWORK, PLUMBING, AIR DISTRIBUTION

10 ELECTRICAL
LIGHTING, CONTROLS, SERVICE & DISTRIBUTION

11 SITEWORK
CLEARING, PAVING, SURFACING, LANDSCAPING

12 GENERAL CONDITIONS & FEES
ARCHITECTURAL/ENGINEERING SERVICES

answer. He could tell you the cost per occupied room in virtually all of his hotels. He knew the difference. He was a remarkable man with a vision and focus that was so unique."

The phenomenal speed at which Gary built hotels and made them profitable, his leadership on Fairfield's franchise advisory board, and the collegial culture he created in the franchise community helped Marriott "transition from a real estate development operating company to a brand company that was very asset-light," said Brown, describing the big shift throughout Marriott. "We spun off all our real estate into a company called Host Marriott, or Host Hotels and Resorts as it's known today, and placed a big emphasis on growing our business with franchisees like Gary."

———————————————

Once Gary started building Marriott hotels, "he understood the value of their brands, I would argue even better than the corporation," said White. "He set the tone to enhance those brands, and other franchisees quickly followed suit."

Remarkably, the tone Gary set created a cohesive franchise community that balanced competition with collaboration.

"It was largely Gary's intellectual capital that produced the new prototypes for each Marriott select-service brand," said White. "As somebody who developed them very aggressively at the time, I know firsthand how his input added tremendous economic value to the projects. Gary made so many people so much money, and I give him credit for setting the tone for the franchise community. Marriott was afraid franchisees were going to erode their brands. But what quickly became apparent was that the franchise community operated with higher standards than Marriott-managed assets did. Gary's influence changed the way Marriott and other franchisors looked at their select-service brands."

White talked about how he was "one of the fortunate ones" because of how willingly Gary shared his experience and expertise. White and his team flew to Fargo from White Lodging's headquarters in suburban Indiana near Chicago. Gary "shared everything with us: his building costs and operating numbers, which were tops in the industry, and how he produced them; his complete building plans; and even the names of subcontractors and sources for materials."

After the visit, White's team kept in touch by phone with peers on Gary's staff until they mastered the Tharaldson method.

Gary's advice was highly valued and constantly sought after by fellow franchisees, not only at the Marriott advisory board meetings, but even more so at conferences, such as the Hunter Hotel Investment Conference and the Goldman Sachs Lodging Conference, and conventions such as the Lodging Conference. Gary also attended annual franchise conferences hosted by Choice, Marriott, Hilton, Carlson and IHG.

By the mid-1990s, "I became somebody they looked up to," Gary recalled. "I heard it all the time from new ones: 'I want to be just like you.' My comment back was, 'That's great, but sometimes that's really hard because of the obstacles in your way. Get one done first, then you can try two, and then maybe four.'"

Even so, building five to 10 hotels a year was rare. "Who does 40 or more?" Gary asked rhetorically with a laugh.

Nor was Gary afraid of "giving away the store." As he put it, "they can know everything I know but I'm still going to beat them."

Once, a fan approached Jascha Heifetz, perhaps the world's greatest violinist ever, to say that the maestro's violin—the 1714 Dolphin Stradivarius—had an incredibly beautiful tone. Heifetz put his ear on the instrument and replied, "I hear nothing."

Gary knew he could play his instrument—the Tharaldson hotel factory—better than anyone else.

As well, as White pointed out, "the hotel industry is very transparent. It all comes down to execution: You need to be good at identifying sites and negotiating deals, but speed to market counts more than anything else. If you're there first with the best product, you win."

Gary was the best by far at getting first to market—and then, often second and third after that.

Because of Gary's generosity with his time and wisdom, many franchisees were able to build and own up to 20 properties during their careers. In Gary's estimation, this would not have happened otherwise.

For example, Rob Uehran, who worked for Gary for six years, went out on his own and now has partial ownership in the hotels owned by Spirit Hospitality, LLC, headquartered in Fort Collins, Colorado. Uehran serves as the President of Acquisitions & Development.

"Gary changed the whole dynamic of how people looked at each other," said White, "and he has never gotten all the credit he deserves."

Marriott franchisees became a cohesive, productive group—as did franchisees at Choice, Hilton, Carlson and IHG, due to Gary's influence. It helped that many franchisees owned brands from more than one company.

It should be noted that these franchisees were, and remain, Type A, driven personalities who are very competitive. "This was very unusual," said White, "and there wasn't any degree of jealousy."

As a result of their relationship, neither White nor Gary looked at each other as competitors. Gary went as far as refusing to compete in the same markets as close friends, and White reciprocated. "If we heard Gary was in a market," White said, "I told my guys to back off, and vice versa." Gary didn't build any hotels in Austin, Texas, for example, until White sold the hotels he built there.

Gary built a Comfort Inn in Austin in 1997 and then backed away as White built 23 hotels there. After White sold these hotels to Robert Johnson, founder and chairman of RLJ Companies, an asset management firm, Gary resumed building there in 2016. Gary has never met Johnson and, according to his developer's code, is free to build without concern. Also, Gary would not consider the JW Marriott in Austin, which White built, to be competition, since it's an upscale, full-service hotel. Similarly, if Gary owned limited service and extended-stay hotels in a city, White could build a fancy hotel without violating their unspoken compact.

Another such friend is Kerry Boekelheide, who founded Summit Hotel Properties in 1990 and ran the company until 2015. At the time, the company's portfolio included 95 hotels in 24 states. Throughout the 1990s, Summit's properties were concentrated in the South and West, where Gary built few properties—except in Texas and California, where there were so many opportunities that coordinating with franchisee friends seldom presented conflicts.

"It's a big country, that's the way we looked at it," Gary and White said in almost the same words. "There's plenty of places to go, so why compete with a friend?"

White emphasized that Gary wasn't helping others out of calculating self-interest. "He didn't actively promote himself. Other franchisees saw what he was doing, and he was very willing to share. As long as Gary thought that person was sincere and would follow up on his advice, he was willing to invest his time. He is a man of great character."

"Gary is a handshake kinda guy," said Brown. "I'm sure he's never even read any of the franchise agreements we sent to him to sign. He trusts that if there's a problem because we misunderstood something, we'll go back and fix it—and of course, we would."

Gary agreed that he trusted Marriott completely and knew they would address any issue even if it wasn't covered in the contract.

White recalled how humble Gary was when he met him and how he stayed that way. "He was the only guy I know in the industry who dressed worse than I did back then," White remarked with a laugh. "He's improved his appearance since then, but I'm still as bad as I ever was."

White remarked that the tone Gary set for the franchisee community was like "that movie that they show at Christmastime every year, 'It's a Wonderful Life.'" Coincidentally, the story on which the film was based was published in Good Housekeeping magazine as "The Man Who Was Never Born" the year Gary was born. The movie was released the next year.

"The franchise community would be radically different if it wasn't for Gary," White concluded.

Understandably, Marriott executives were cautious about entering the franchise business, as they expressed at the meeting of original franchisees in 1991. Gary's example and influence allayed their anxieties and paved the way for over 900 Marriott franchisees worldwide today. At first, the fees Marriott collected from franchisees amounted to only a small part of the company's revenue. Since then, Marriott's franchise income has increased to $11 billion, which is 65 percent of its revenue worldwide ($17 billion) and 50 percent of its income in the Americas in 2016.

Brown characterized Gary's story as "the epitome of the American dream. He built a terrific business in North Dakota with a great culture. Many people have worked with him for a long time, and that's the sign of great leadership that inspires followership. People stay with you for the culture you create and the opportunities you provide. Gary has certainly done that over his career."

Culture is one of the most important drivers of sustainable success. More than money, "it's why people stay in a company and also why they leave," said Brown. As with the Tharaldson companies, Marriott has maintained one of the lowest turnover rates in the industry.

The Marriott and Tharaldson cultures were so in sync that managerial training for Gary's Marriott hotels was carried out at the Tharaldson training center. The same was true for his Choice hotels. Gary converted the second (top) floor of his Econo Lodge in Fargo to a management training facility, with a lecture hall, a business library and computer labs outfitted with the property management systems for the hotel brands the company operated. In addition, managers received in-depth training in Tharaldson corporate culture and that of the hotel company whose brand or brands they would operate.

This practice made sense until the early 2000s, when Gary's building pace slowed down. Then it was more economical to pay $20,000 to have a manager trained at Marriott's training center in Bethesda, Maryland. Gary never built enough Hilton or IHG hotels to justify training managers completely at his training facility.

"The service industry is the largest vocational trainer in the United States of America. We take people with limited skills, like me," said Brown, "and teach them the business from the bottom up. They go from minimum wage to a solid middle income and beyond. It's the immigrant story and the American dream story. Sixty percent of our managers come from the lower ranks and we're terribly proud of that."

Everyone at Tharaldson Enterprises has a similar story. For example, Dobmeier began as a bookkeeper and Fyke as a hotel manager. They have enjoyed highly successful careers and become wealthy. Lori Kasowski started working for Gary 25 years ago as an office assistant to become an office manager who will retire in comfort.

As Gary put it, "We don't have degrees in this stuff. We're just a company that goes on our gut instinct, and when it isn't working we make adjustments." Actually, Fyke earned a bachelor's degree in hospitality management, which Gary has forgotten if he ever knew it—but that is the only academic qualification in lodging in any of Gary's companies. And clearly, it is the only degree the Tharaldson companies needed.

———————

As Gary got to know Marriott from the inside, he was very impressed with how professional everyone was who worked there, from desk clerks to executives. In typical fashion, Gary incorporated the essence of Marriott's culture into his companies and gave back to Marriott the best of Tharaldson company culture.

Marriott executives learned how to think with precision about building and operational efficiencies, which allowed Marriott to flourish as a franchisor in the select-service and extended-stay lodging sectors. Although Gary and his team dress less formally than Marriott's personnel, they measure up to the same level of professionalism. Most importantly, the two company cultures are the same at heart.

"Gary's hotel employees wear our uniform and represent us, too," said Brown. "It's vitally important for us to have franchisees who share our values in terms of how they treat people and run their company. We are dedicated to the customer through service excellence—and this includes internal customers such as our franchisees. We believe in a true partnership, as does Gary."

Brown emphasized that the Marriott corporation had the same humble origins as did the Tharaldson companies. "Our founder, J.W. Marriott, Sr., started by opening a nine-seat root beer stand in Washington, D.C.," he said. "That's the foundation of the company, and we haven't forgotten it." Brown noted that Mr. Marriott, Sr., had a line he repeated that became the cornerstone of his hotel empire: "Take care of your people and they'll take care of the customers. The customers will come back and we all make money."

It's not surprising that Marriott pioneered guest satisfaction surveys in the hospitality industry. When Marriott established its Fairfield brand, it installed scorecard terminals in hotel lobbies for customers to rate their experience. The

Marriott International, Inc.   Marriott Drive
Corporate Headquarters   Washington, D.C. 20058

J. Willard Marriott, Jr.
Chairman of the Board
and Chief Executive Officer
301/380-7511
301/380-8957 Fax

November 30, 1998

Mr. Gary Tharaldson
Tharaldson Enterprises
1202 Westrac Drive, SW
Fargo, North Dakota 58103

Dear Gary:

Congratulations on opening your 100th Fairfield Inn! This is truly an exciting and important milestone for Tharaldson Enterprises. I regret I could not attend the celebration in Fargo to congratulate you personally.

As you take this time to celebrate your growth and success, please know we value your business and are delighted that you decided to work with us in the building of your Fairfield Inn's throughout the country. We look forward to working with you on your upcoming openings in 1999.

I understand you spoke very positively about your experiences with Marriott when you participated in a press briefing last month at our Owners Conference in Palm Springs. I appreciate your quotes in *The Washington Post* article on November 16th stating you were "Bullish" on our new SpringHill Suites brand.

You have been an important franchisee over the years, and we look forward to many more years of working together. Again, congratulations on this tremendous accomplishment!

Warmest regards,

J.W. Marriott, Jr.

company's objective was to distinguish itself in the limited-service market by providing excellent customer service. Also not surprising is the fact that Gary's hotels achieve the highest customer satisfaction scores across all the Marriott brands he franchised.

Both J.W. Marriott and his son Bill Marriott were notorious for interrupting hotel inspections to talk with employees, from maids to general managers—but especially with those at the bottom of the corporate ladder. "Like his father, Mr. Marriott stopped to talk to every employee in a hallway or wherever he visited," said Dobmeier about Bill Marriott's presence at the opening of Gary's first Residence Inn in Appleton, Wisconsin, in 1992. "He talked to them about their families and was very personable."

Dobmeier also remarked that Gary has many of the same characteristics as Mr. Marriott. "He's got a million things going through his mind, but when we traveled to our hotels, he always took the time to visit with employees. He was always very sensitive to that and it was very important."

One of the integral ways Gary built a vibrant and attractive culture for his companies was through life-work-family balance. As White commented, "I was a more traditional hotel developer, running all over the country all the time to find new sites and hands-on manage our hotels. Meanwhile, Gary was playing a lot of softball and spending his summers at his lake home with his family. He taught me a lot about how to organize myself, set priorities and delegate effectively. He had some incredibly effective management skills."

Although Gary opened a new hotel every fortnight on average throughout the 1990s, he almost never missed a sporting event or performance involving his children. He went to hundreds of baseball, basketball, football, soccer and hockey games—most of which started in the late afternoon.

"I want a full life," said Gary. "It's not all about business." He tells his employees to do the same. "I know you work hard and the work will get done, so if you need to leave early for a family event or a kid's game, do so," he would say. "Your kids are only young once." Without having to be told, his employees always responded by finishing tasks later in the evening when necessary.

"I learned that I could not build a big company without trusting a lot of good people," said Gary. "I step in to manage if they're making a mistake." Otherwise Gary acts like a coach for his executives and managers, who know their jobs well now but still need direction on occasion. Mostly they simply need reassurance. "Sometimes being a good coach is being a good cheerleader and letting people know that they're doing a great job," Gary said. "You never can give too much praise. It's very important for people to know that you like what they're doing."

If Gary wrote an employee handbook, it would resemble the one-page edition at Nordstrom, Inc. This upscale department store chain is renowned for superior customer service. Its employee handbook consists of a single card that reads: "Use good judgment in all situations." This trust translates into better morale and higher retention rates.

Nordstrom has often been listed in Fortune Magazine's 100 Best Companies to Work For. The page for the Great Places to Work certification process on Fortune's website states: "Decades of research shows [sic] workplaces with high-trust cultures see higher levels of innovation, customer and patient satisfaction, employee engagement, organizational agility, and more."

Brown described a business council meeting in 2017 at which Bill Marriott, who was 85 years old at the time, was asked what he is most proud of in his life and career. "As I reflect back on my life," Marriott said, "what I am most proud of is the opportunity I had to help and provide for people. And if there's one thing I want to be remembered for, it is that my parents gave me an opportunity to grow, develop and run this business, and I want people to say the same about me: that I gave people an opportunity to grow as individuals, to grow their careers, to develop their business skills, and that I provide them with an opportunity to succeed in the world."

Brown likened Gary to Bill Marriott, saying, "he brought a very powerful, compelling focus on business, on taking care of customers and on taking care of his people. Gary created a huge number of jobs, and the ESOP he set up is a tremendous story of how much money his employees eventually made."

Big Giveaway,
Bigger Headache,
Biggest Score

1998-2006

CHAPTER NINE

Best Decision

Being good in business is the most
fascinating kind of art. Making money
is art and working is art and good
business is the best art.

Andy Warhol

IN THE FALL OF 1997, Gary initiated the refinancing of 189 hotels with the Goldman Sachs Group, Inc., an investment banking company headquartered in New York City. Goldman Sachs' valuation of these properties at about $544 million surprised Gary. He had always calculated the worth of his hotels very conservatively—in keeping with his Midwestern ethos. New Yorkers are certainly more aggressive and Goldman Sachs analysts concluded that these hotels were worth about 25 percent more than Gary had calculated.

The following February, the deal closed for $363 million (at 60 percent of Goldman Sachs' valuation). The purpose of the refinancing was to secure lower interest rates on existing debt, improve cash flow and free up capital to invest in building new hotels.

Now that Goldman Sachs was well aware of Gary's hospitality empire, they would return in eight years with an offer, chronicled in the next chapter, that would astound Gary and lead to the most colorful—albeit harrowing—period of his career.

In 1997, a journalistic powerhouse that has made much of its impact via lists took notice of Gary, too. In the October issue of Forbes magazine, Gary was ranked number 395 on the Forbes 400, which is the annual list of the 400 wealthiest Americans. Getting on the list had been one of Gary's personal goals since it was first published in 1982—coincidently, the year he bought his first two hotels. He was featured in a thumbnail photo on the front cover as one of the 30 new members of the Forbes 400. Gary's net worth was listed as $485 million.

Gary "[n]ow has 235 hotels," Forbes reported. "Occupancy 10 percent above and break-even points 10 percent below industry averages." The magazine also noted that he "[s]huns the high life: houses in Fargo and Phoenix cost about $300,000 apiece." Prophetically, Forbes stated that Gary "thinks Wall Street money is foolish: 'I'll get to a billion, but I'll do it my way—and I'll own it all.'"

Gary made the list again the following year, ranked at number 385 with a net worth of $520 million. Forbes described him as the "[r]ichest man in South Dakota." Oops, that honor belonged to Theodore Waitt, who founded Gateway, Inc., a computer hardware company. Now Gary's hotel count was up to 290 and Forbes correctly mentioned that he "dines at Red Lobster in Fargo."

Making the Forbes 400 was an amazing accomplishment for anyone, let alone a kid who grew up between Nowhere and Nothing, North Dakota. The entire state doesn't even rank as flyover country. Rather it's flyover country for people from proverbial flyover regions, such as Minnesota and Iowa. Now Gary was making as much in a minute as his father did in two days of hard work after adjusting for inflation.

As would be true year after year, Forbes underestimated his net worth, which has never bothered Gary. "I don't lose a penny when they get it wrong," he said with a smile.

Gary seemed destined to make it onto the list of The World's Billionaires, which Forbes first published in 1987. By 2000, there were 477 billionaires on the planet with an average net worth of $1.9 billion. Given Gary's competitive nature and his relentless pace of building new hotels regardless of economic ups and downs, his net worth was bound to double and then triple within several years. As well, Gary had a habit of quickly establishing himself as above average in any business setting. Surpassing the $1.9 billion mark was within a decade's striking distance.

Gary was accumulating softball trophies and hospitality awards that would fill a warehouse, which demonstrated how dearly he loved to win and how much it hurt to lose.

Maybe he would have tried to best fellow Nevadan Sheldon Adelson, the current chairman and CEO of Las Vegas Sands Corporation. Like Gary, Adelson started with nothing, in his case, as the son of immigrant parents living in a Boston tenement. Adelson's net worth in 1997 was $550 million, about 13 percent greater than Gary's—which is close in their world. By 2016, Adelson was valued at $30.4 billion.

Nor was the personal net worth of Bill Marriott, at $810 million, massively different from Gary's in 1997. The thing about wealth is that once a critical mass is achieved, a point that varies according to industry, net worth can increase at fantastic rates.

For example, Kirk Kerkorian, a billionaire investor, made $660 million in a single day when Chrysler announced its intention to merge with Daimler-Benz in May 1998. That year, Steve Jobs was worth $1 billion—58 times less than Bill Gates. Forbes calculated that Jobs would have been worth $31.6 billion at the time of his death in 2011 "if he held all of his initial [Apple]

Gary with Steve Forbes, the publisher of Forbes magazine, at a Choice Hotels International Annual Convention in the mid-1990s.

shares." Those shares were worth $50.56 billion a year later. Meanwhile, Gates' net worth had fallen to $49 billion in 2011. Such are the ups and downs of vast fortunes, which can resemble trampoline trajectories—both fascinating and enticing for someone as confident as Gary.

It's important to note that the self-made members of the 2016 Forbes 400 account for two-thirds of the entire list's aggregate net worth of $2.4 trillion. In fact, most of the people we think of as the wealthiest Americans are self-made, including Bill Gates, Jeff Bezos, Warren Buffet, Mark Zuckerberg and Larry Ellison, who take the top five spots.

Instead of trying to play in the financial major leagues with his mostly self-made colleagues, Gary could have cashed out and retired to play his beloved softball full-time and spend more time with family as his younger children and grandchildren grew up.

Gary didn't choose to cash out, of course. He was having too much fun, as he never tires of saying—always as if he's never said it before. This is because building hotels and orchestrating his business in ever-widening arcs across the country is a daily rediscovery of joy. Gary delights in the deep sense that he is doing exactly what God created him to do.

Robert Orben—a magician, comedy writer and speechwriter for Vice President Gerald R. Ford, hopefully in that order—wrote: "Every day I get up and look through the Forbes list of the richest people in America. If I'm not there, I go to work." What happens when one wakes up and finds oneself on the list?

Astoundingly, Gary didn't choose to join the billionaires either—at least not yet. He had something far more important to do.

As a point of clarification, until the refinancing in 1998, Gary's companies were part of Tharaldson Enterprises. Goldman Sachs told Gary to make sure that all his various companies were legally separated, for liability reasons. From then on, they were referred to as the Tharaldson companies or "The Company"—not to be confused, however, with the CIA.

The question that had bothered Gary deeply long before the refinancing and making the Forbes 400 was how to take care of the futures of all 6,500 full-time employees across the country. Hotel managers, construction foremen and other mid-rank employees had the typical 401(k) retirement plans and would end their careers with modest incomes in retirement. That was far from satisfactory for Gary. Central to his mission as an entrepreneur was to make those who devoted themselves to realizing his dreams in the hospitality industry as wealthy as possible.

In the early 1990s, Gary set up a plan to take care of his top people and those he worked with daily at the Fargo headquarters. He gave each of these employees, numbering 20 in total, 4 percent of the stock in a specific hotel after three and a half years of service. Senior management earned percentages in more than one hotel.

In order to complete the Goldman Sachs refinancing, Gary was required to buy back all this stock for cash or a promissory note. Only one employee cashed out right away and left to work elsewhere (a rare occurrence). She told

Gary she had never had that much money and never dreamed she would. The cash-out was life-changing and she was most grateful. To everyone else in the plan, Gary issued a 20-year note at 9 percent interest per annum. In addition to semi-annual checks ranging from $5,000 to almost $70,000 for 20 years, each of the remaining 14 participants are scheduled to receive a final payout in 2018, ranging from about $50,000 to $1.4 million. One executive cashed out in 2016 for over $2 million.

After the refinancing deal was complete, Gary could have created a new plan going forward for those close to him. "But what about the cleaning maids, clerks and other hourly workers?" Gary asked himself repeatedly. Like his parents, they worked hard for years while they raised families and often sent money back to Mexico or Poland, for example. In retirement, they would have little more than Social Security to live on—just as Gary's parents would have fared had he not become successful enough to take care of them. Nor would his brothers and sisters have enjoyed affluence—which was not about indulgence in the Tharaldson clan but about an enjoyable lifestyle and, most importantly, about providing for children and grandchildren to ensure that every family member had the opportunity to attend college or whatever preparation he or she needed to start a successful career.

He could have simply paid everyone more, but compensation rates were already on par with or exceeding industry standards. The employees would also have to pay income tax at normal rates and this loss of capital would greatly hamper Gary's ability to grow the company. The equity for hotel development to this point was entirely self-generated. Then profits from hotel operations were re-invested in building and opening new properties. Fewer hotels would mean far fewer jobs and less revenue.

By August 1998, Gary decided that an employee stock ownership plan (ESOP) would be the best option. In short, an ESOP involves setting up a trust into which some to all profits are deposited. Then the trust funds are used to buy the company in whole or in part. Often, an ESOP starts with the owner selling one third to one half of the company to the employees to ease the financial burden of the purchase. Sometimes, it might take 20 years for the company to become completely owned by the workers, or the ESOP might become a partnership with the owner and remain at partial ownership.

Four of the important benefits an ESOP offers are:

1. There are no upfront costs for the employees. Although setting up the ESOP might cost as much as $250,000 in legal and other fees, the owner pays these. Whatever percentage of the company the employees buy, the purchase amount comes totally out of profits going forward.

2. The owner pays no tax on the transfer of ownership since the employees won't begin to pay for the company until after acquiring their share of ownership.

3. As long as the employees are buying more than 30 percent of the company, capital gains taxes are deferred completely, with the proviso that any investments from profits are made in American companies.

4. An ESOP supplies a succession plan. The central idea here is that people who know the company and the industry best are the ones who end up running the company. They also have an acutely vested interest in long-term sustainability and growth.

Gary originally intended the ESOP to own 50 percent of a company called Tharaldson Motels Incorporated (TMI), which was created in 1993. By August 1998, TMI included 204 hotels with about 15,000 rooms. However, the firm Gary hired to set up the ESOP failed to complete the transaction properly. In keeping with his decisive and somewhat impatient nature, Gary chose to sell the entire company to the ESOP, which totaled 214 hotels in December 1999 when the ESOP was finalized.

Gary still owned 82 hotels, not included in the ESOP, and he had 19 under construction that would open in 2000. In fact, part of the ESOP arrangement was that Gary would continue building hotels as before—with the employees who now owned TMI via the ESOP—and he would pay TMI fees to develop and manage the new hotels. TMI would not develop any new hotels but instead would manage their 214 properties.

ESOPs are becoming a more common corporate phenomenon. A national survey in 2010 showed that 17.4 percent of private sector employees owned various forms (including ESOPs) of stock or stock options in their companies, according to the National Center for Employee Ownership. There are currently about 6,800 ESOPs nationwide involving 13.9 million participants.

When Gary set up TMI's ESOP, he vowed "to make it the best one in the U.S." It would not be the largest. Publix Super Markets, which establish an ESOP in 1974, enjoys that distinction with 182,500 employees. Gary's ESOP would currently rank about 35th in size. Would it be the best? Time and betrayal would have their say before the answer was reached.

Management is critical to an ESOP's long-term success. If the company is not well-run, the value of shares in profits will be seriously jeopardized, putting the ESOP and the company at risk of failure. ESOPs come with substantial risk, in that economic downturns can depress revenues and seriously downgrade the value of a company. A deep, prolonged recession can threaten the very existence of a company and therefore employee retirement funds.

Gary believed firmly that in this case, there was no risk since he remained at the helm ready to deal with any challenges. Gary stayed on as the plan's trustee. "I didn't want another CEO to come and screw it up," he said. Gary took no salary for his daily involvement in steering TMI. He did, however, receive a consulting fee of $1.6 million per year for his services, out of which he paid for several employees who worked directly for him regarding TMI's affairs. What he cleared at the end of the year amounted to no more than a normal salary.

As noted earlier, Gary had set up his companies to weather distress. His breakeven point was lower and his organization was lean, nimble and highly proficient. If TMI failed, he would never see the outstanding $444.46 million and would be liable for TMI's $400 million in bank debt, which he guaranteed. The biggest risk was to Gary's economic well-being, but he never gave that a first thought, let alone a second glance.

The ESOP fit well with the paradoxical nature of Gary's leadership. On the one hand, Gary remained the main decision-maker, which instilled confidence among employees that the ESOP would work out well. On the other hand, as Gary had learned years earlier, empowering his managers produced the best results and working atmosphere. He wanted employees to make decisions and take ownership of their jobs. He believed he prepared them well for their responsibilities and then let them go to stand and sometimes fall flat. Gary could endure failures as long as these served as learning experiences. Also, his managers were given a very clear sense of objectives and best practices. It

Gary signs documents creating the ESOP in December 1999. Behind him are crutches since he had just undergone an osteotomy on his left knee to realign the joint properly.

helped greatly that Gary was available 24/7 for consultation and made quick decisions.

On December 27, 1999, the ESOP took 100 percent ownership of all of TMI's common stock. TMI received an independent valuation of $1 billion. This consisted mostly of the outstanding debt on the hotels ($400 million) and Gary's equity ($510 million). At the transaction's close, Gary received $50 million in cash to continue developing hotels and took a promissory note for $444.46 million. These notes were divided into nine different classes with staggered maturity dates, which ranged from 19.5 to 31 years.

Since 150 hotels in the TMI portfolio were part of the Goldman Sachs refinancing deal, most of the outstanding debt on the hotels ($400 million) was financed long-term at rates significantly lower than the fixed rate at the time. "This created a significant cash flow advantage for ESOP," Gary was very pleased to say. In short, the advantages that Gary negotiated with the Goldman Sachs refinancing were largely passed on to the ESOP.

Gary had the option of including himself and his brothers and sisters in the ESOP, since they worked for him in various capacities. However, he chose not to do so. "I did it for the employees," he said, "I did it as the best way of sharing the wealth. I did it because I love to do it."

In summary, Gary gave his employees a $1 billion company for no money down. Also, before creating the ESOP, Gary was using $80 million of TMI's funds principally to build new hotels, which was the normal procedure. Since the new properties were not destined to be owned by TMI (although, again, they would be developed and managed by TMI for a fee), Gary set up a repayment schedule, which was fulfilled.

As the new millennium dawned, Gary was set to go forward on two fronts: building his second empire and managing the ESOP portfolio. Seemingly he had accomplished his goal regarding his employees and still had all the same top people in place to build his second lodging empire: Larson was in charge of construction, Dobmeier and Fyke were running operations, and Annette Croves managed accounting and human resources.

A now-obscure book was published in 1993—*Finding Your Strength in Difficult Times: A Book of Meditations*—with a famous, albeit often misquoted saying. The book's author, Dr. David Viscott, was a psychiatrist and popular radio talk-show host in Los Angeles in the 1980s and 1990s "who provided diagnoses and 'tough love' therapy," according to his New York Times obituary. Gary never read Viscott's books nor listened to his broadcasts, but these words capture the arc of Gary's career from buying two hotels in 1982 to setting up the ESOP in 1999:

The purpose of life is to discover your gift.
The work of life is to develop it.
The meaning of life is to give your gift away.

———————

Every year, wealthy individuals account for most of the nation's philanthropy: The wealthy accounted for 72 percent of the $390 billion given to U.S. charities in 2016, according to "Giving USA 2017: The Annual Report on Philanthropy for the Year 2016." This generosity does society a tremendous amount of good. The two top recipients of philanthropic largesse are religious institutions (32 percent) and educational institutions (15 percent).

In fact, 158 of the world's wealthy have signed the "Giving Pledge," which is a promise to give away most of their fortunes to philanthropic causes. The campaign was founded by Bill Gates and Warren Buffett. Other billionaire signatories include Harold Hamm, Sara Blakely and Richard Branson.

Gary has also donated millions of dollars, mostly to educational institutions both secular and faith-based, and he will continue to do so. However, traditional philanthropy is not the only way business becomes a force for good in society. Nor is charity the primary means.

By 2011, Gates had given away a third of his fortune ($28 billion) and fallen out of first place on the billionaires' list. Before giving away a penny, Gates had to found his company and make $75 billion. In doing so, he created thousands of jobs—and Steve Jobs, in a significant sense. Microsoft's success created the need and incentive for competition. To borrow a simplified yet useful analogy, Microsoft appealed to left-brained, analytic people and businesses, while Apple appealed far more to right-brained, creative people and businesses. Accounting firms use Microsoft programs and graphics firms use Apple products. These two techno-giants created tens of thousands of jobs, directly and indirectly, and trillions of dollars in wealth, directly and indirectly.

To illustrate, let's suppose that Gates donated $28 billion to various colleges and universities. This would constitute an enormously helpful gift to these schools. However, it is businesses such as his that provide the jobs that make it possible for people to earn a living, marry and raise children, and then have the resources to pay tuition, room and board and other expenses—which amount to much more than $28 billion.

Similarly, Gary contributes far more to society through his companies—providing jobs, services and tax revenue—than giving money away could ever accomplish. Gary's made thousands of families affluent, including more than 100 achieving millionaire status. These families were given the opportunity to raise the next generation with both the means and time off work to practice good parenting. These families have contributed and continue to contribute their time and treasure to their communities, churches, schools and associations across the country. These families passed on Gary's generosity in widening spheres. As G.K. Chesterton observed, "Too much capitalism does not mean too many capitalists, but too few capitalists."

The philanthropy that wealthy individuals like Gary practice via charitable giving is invaluable but still the smaller part of the story of how society is served directly and indirectly by such business leaders. The question is how to best balance this and how to set up a succession plan that keeps such businesses robust after current leadership departs.

Gary shies away from public attention, as do many entrepreneurs who build companies. There is much in the media about a relative few business leaders. Most business dynamos, however, shrink from personal limelight. Perhaps what Confucius wrote 2,500 years ago still applies: "It is the way of the superior man to prefer the concealment of his virtue, while it daily becomes more illustrious, and it is the way of the mean man to seek notoriety, while he daily goes more and more to ruin."

CHAPTER TEN

Worst Decision

No good deed goes unpunished.

Everybody Else

Today is the pupil of yesterday.

Publilius

AS THE ESOP was being established throughout 1999, Gary opened 28 new hotels and also had 19 hotels in the construction pipeline. Six of the hotels that opened in 1999 were included in the TMI ESOP portfolio. The rest of the 1999 hotels became part of Gary's portfolio, along with all hotels built in subsequent years. These new hotels included the last five Choice hotels Gary ever constructed, which were two Comfort Inns, two Comfort Suites and one Comfort Inn & Suites. As mentioned in the previous chapter, Gary thought very highly of Choice hotels, but Marriott brands especially offered the most room for growth in the upscale select- and extended-stay sector.

Eighty-eight percent of the 101 hotels he built from 1999 through 2005 were Marriott (75) and Hilton (13) properties in seven brands (five Marriott and two Hilton). Gary continued to build Fairfield hotels, constructing 20 over this seven-year period, but he was clearly easing out of this brand. In fact, after 2005, he built only two Fairfields, one in 2006 and the other in 2016.

From 1982 through 2005, Gary built 394 hotels. He also purchased 18, for a total of 412 hotels, a breathtaking number of properties for a private hotel developer starting with modest capital. During these years, Gary sold for cash or swapped 62 hotels for land to develop new properties, leaving 350 hotels in total in TMI's and his portfolio, all of which he and his top managers were running. The cash from hotel sales went directly into developing new properties.

At the end of 2005, TMI was managing 350 hotels: 200 hotels owned by the ESOP and 150 hotels owned by Gary. The size of the hotels was gradually getting larger. The average room size of the TMI hotels, which included more of the older hotels in the overall portfolio, was 68 rooms. In comparison, the hotels Gary owned at the time had 83 rooms on average. In total, the portfolio had 25,983 rooms in 36 states: 13,563 rooms in TMI hotels and 12,420 rooms in Gary's hotels.

The increase in hotel size and focus on more upscale brands were due to Gary building in larger urban centers surrounded by more affluent neighborhoods. Land costs were much higher, but the return on investment was greater still. This shift in focus also accounts for the smaller number of hotels constructed after 1999. These were also recessionary years, which naturally dampens output. The only down year was 2005, when only four hotels were built. At this time, Gary was concentrating most of his energies on the prospective sale of all 350 hotels.

In July 2000, Gary opened a 78-room Fairfield in North Little Rock, Arkansas. A month later, he opened a much larger Residence Inn (96 rooms) next door. That year, there were about 60,000 residents in North Little Rock, where Jerry Jones, the billionaire owner of the Dallas Cowboys, grew up. Jones was born three years before Gary, almost to the day. In 1998, Jones's net worth was $525 million, only $5 million more than Gary's.

North Little Rock is located just across the Arkansas River from the state capital, Little Rock, which had about 183,000 residents at the time; there were more than 700,000 people in the metropolitan area. Gary's hotels are located beside an exit from Interstate Highway 40, which connects directly to Memphis and Nashville, Tennessee, to the east, and to Oklahoma City, Oklahoma, to the west. The exit leads past Gary's Residence Inn and Fairfield Inn to the region's major medical campus, the Baptist Health Medical Center, which is within walking distance. There is a mall nearby and several big box stores, such as Walmart, and the area is surrounded by upscale neighborhoods.

In Rancho Cucamonga, California, Gary opened a 103-room Homewood Suites on November 22, 2005. On the same site, Gary had two additional hotels under construction: his first Hilton Garden Inn, which opened on February 13, 2006, and has 122 rooms; and a Courtyard Inn, which opened June 29, 2006, and has 117 rooms.

Interestingly, Hilton Garden Suites and Courtyard Inns typically have restaurants in-house that serve breakfast and dinner. In fact, this is usually part of the franchise agreement. However, Gary found that running a restaurant in the evenings for guests only, since people not staying at the hotels seldom dined at these venues, was a tremendous expenditure of energy and expertise for no financial return. Although restaurants are often located in hotels, Gary has learned that food service is an entirely different business than running a hotel. "I would rather give food away as a continental breakfast than try to run restaurants," he said. Now his Courtyards and Hilton Garden Inns serve only breakfast as a sit-down meal. There is bar service available in the evenings.

Rancho Cucamonga is a city of mostly upscale suburbs with about 137,000 residents in 2005. The city is located about 37 miles east of downtown Los Angeles in the foothills of the San Gabriel Mountains. Snowcapped peaks rising above the desert landscape provide spectacular views. The median household income in Rancho Cucamonga was about $78,000, and the per-family median income was more than $90,000. The city was ranked 42nd on Money magazine's "Best Places to Live" list. Also, one of Rancho Cucamonga's many gated communities, Haven View Estates, was listed at number 13 on Business Insider's "The 27 Richest Neighborhoods in Southern California."

Gary's three hotels in Rancho Cucamonga are located across from a major shopping mall in Ontario, near the Ontario International Airport and the interchange of two major interstates, I-10 and I-15. To build the hotels, Gary bought all of the property bound by four streets. He subdivided the site into several retail lots (currently with five stores and four restaurants), which he sold for enough to cover the cost of the land he used to build the hotels.

Gary has covered land costs in this manner several times before and continues to look for this opportunity. In fact, he is currently building two hotels—a Staybridge Suites and a Home2 Suites by Hilton (a mid-scale extended-stay brand)—side by side, only one mile west of the Rancho Cucamonga properties. There, too, Gary is selling land for retail and other projects that will pay for the land he is using for the hotels. In this area of California, these deals save him $3 million per hotel.

The only risk in building in Rancho Cucamonga is earthquake damage. The city sits only 20 miles from San Bernardino, which is located right above the main branch of the San Andreas fault line. Clearly, it's no accident that the city's minor-league baseball team was named the Rancho Cucamonga Quakes, and the team mascot (who would have guessed?) was called Tremor. Oh, the stadium was originally named the Epicenter. Hopefully, the Pacific and North American plates have a sense of humor as they slide across each other: safe on second!

Gary entered the new century with 19 hotels under construction in 11 states. He was happily building his second hotel empire and, most importantly, feeling great about solving his fundamental moral issue in his businesses with the ESOP: how to take care of all of his full-time employees.

It soon became clear that the ESOP was giving TMI and Gary's companies a distinct competitive advantage. Recruiting and retaining the best employees became significantly easier, Dobmeier attested.

"Our turnover probably went from 40 percent to less than 20 percent after the ESOP," he said, indicating that this included cleaning maids and janitors. "When our employees started to get statements about their stock prices, they got interested. And then when they saw their stock price double from five to ten dollars, they really started to pay attention."

At this point, the employees "realized they were now the new owners," said Dobmeier. "Soon I felt like I was working for thousands of people as my boss. Their attitudes changed and it was very positive." The employees started acting like owners and took more responsibility for the hotels they worked in, not only for their specific jobs but also for operations as a whole. "As they saw how much value their shares had, they supported that, as owners, everyone's performance, regardless of position, makes a difference in our business being successful."

By the end of the ESOP's first year, Dobmeier's view became standard attitudinal procedure: "None of us employees paid anything for what was given to us via the ESOP. So, what we had to do was manage it and make it profitable, and that's what we did."

TMI's stock price increased steadily to $36.50 a share in 2008. Then the Great Recession hit and stock prices became a roller coaster. Over the next two years, the price dropped as low as $17.

"How do you go out and explain to a housekeeper who is making minimum wage that her value just dropped in half?" Dobmeier recalled his morale problem during the recession. "They are not in the stock market and don't understand it. These were difficult times to keep people fired up about their jobs and to have confidence that the company would get back on track."

Economic ups and downs are parts of recurring cycles, and Dobmeier recalled four of them in his tenure. This was the worst one, and it required that he and the other vice presidents, as well as the regional vice presidents, area directors and individual hotel managers, allay their employees' worries and inspire top performance in the face of temporary setbacks—as owners. Their salaries, of course, were not affected.

Back in 2001, the Great Recession was not on anyone's mind, not only at Gary's companies but nationwide. Instead, businesses were dealing with the milder U-shaped recession that started in the second quarter of 2000 and lasted until the third quarter of 2003. A U-shaped recession, according to Samuel Johnson, a former chief economist at the International Monetary Fund, is like a bathtub: "You go in. You stay in. The sides are slippery. You know, maybe there's some bumpy stuff in the bottom, but you don't come out of the bathtub for a long time."

For Gary, economic downturns had rarely been a consideration—other than as an advantage. While competitors struggled, for example, after the mini-crash in global stock markets in 1997, which was caused by an economic crisis in Asia, Gary kept building as if nothing had happened.

From then until the second quarter of 2001, an historic financial bubble swelled because of excess speculation on Internet stocks. The dot-com collapse shook the economy and the U-shaped recession, mentioned above, took hold.

Then the savage terrorist attacks on September 11, 2001, had an immediate and long-lasting effect on the hotel sector. There was a significant drop in occupancy rates that lasted for three months. Nationwide, the RevPar (explained on page 165) fell by 20 to 25 percent.

Still, Gary's economic model held. Although he slowed down his building pace, it was much faster than any other private hotel developer. This was especially fortunate for employees at TMI and Gary's other companies. In February 2001, the unemployment rate stood at 4.2 percent, which would be the lowest rate until June 2017. Then, 1.735 million jobs were lost beginning in March 2001, and the unemployment rate increased to 6.3 percent by June 2003. Gary's employees didn't need to worry about losing their jobs because of economic downturns.

A thousand years before Confucius, a cryptic saying was inscribed in stone at a temple in Luxor, Egypt: "No joy without pain." No doubt in another temple yet to be discovered is a companion saying: "The bigger the joy, the bigger the pain."

During the first months of 2000, Gary visited hotels celebrating the ESOP with employees and explaining relevant details. It was a time of happiness and inner peace. Gary had done well and then done good. All was in balance and the future for this 55-year-old seemed glaringly bright. His net worth was over $700 million. Granted, over $400 million of that was in long-term notes from the ESOP, but Gary had no worries about being paid. He looked forward to building a second empire with the same people who had helped build his first one. Eventually they would all retire comfortably with their families well taken care of.

On June 29, 2001, Gary sent a letter to a longtime employee and friend terminating a business agreement. Within two weeks, the employee filed a lawsuit. Since Gary does not want to embarrass the man, he will not be referred to by name, nor will this lawsuit be discussed in detail. It was eventually resolved and the plaintiff ended up with what he would have gotten anyway.

Looking back on the scenario, Gary said it was a disagreement between friends that got out of hand and if they had gotten together and talked it out, they would have reached a resolution. Gary had already made this man and his wife quite affluent, something he would likely not have accomplished on his own. As well, if he had accepted Gary's letter and done nothing, he was going to make several million dollars from the current deal and then would have earned millions of dollars more from future work. Filing the lawsuit, clearly, should have been a last resort, not the first response.

The dynamic of any discord usually changes for the worse when lawyers are brought in. This suit was no exception. To be clear, the lawsuit had nothing whatever to do with the ESOP.

At year's end, the lawsuit was a minor annoyance for Gary. But as any migraine sufferer knows well, that's how massive headaches begin: a small twinge behind the eyes or in one of temples, a feeling of disorientation or slight nausea. Eventually, pain sets in and grows, often spreading and immobilizing.

Gary's old friend was about to give him a whopper of a legal migraine, to the point where Gary said, "The ESOP was the best decision I ever made and the worst decision."

Four years later, this lawsuit had not been settled. Nor did Gary feel any pressure to get it out of the way. He believed he was in the right and was ready to go to trial if necessary, not that he thought about it much. It was an annoying blip on his daily radar screen, but no more than that—or so he assumed.

However, his onetime friend and the friend's wife were thinking about it, as the man would tell Gary years later. The couple was stewing in anger, which precipitated a scheme to force tens of millions of dollars out of Gary.

As he told Gary several years later, the lawyers that he and his wife hired proposed a plan to squeeze money out of Gary from another direction, since their litigation was stalled. The lawyers hit on the idea of finding one or more disgruntled former employees and using them as the platform to launch a class-action lawsuit regarding the ESOP. The suit would not bring significant reward to Gary's former friend. But that was not the intent. The lawsuit could cost Gary dearly and, not coincidentally, provide a huge windfall for the lawyers.

The case—Hans, et al. v. Tharaldson, et al.—was filed on December 29, 2005. The suit alleged that Gary caused the TMI ESOP to overpay for a highly risky company that was declining in value with a portfolio of obsolete hotels.

However, the RevPar results and the EBITDA performance (on the following page) clearly demonstrate that the TMI hotels were increasing in value and therefore far from obsolete.

In fact, the RevPar at the 200 TMI hotels, in comparison to competing hotels in the same marketing sectors (select-service and extended-stay), was remarkable. RevPar is a common performance metric in the hospitality industry used to measure and benchmark operating performance. The information to determine RevPar and other metrics is collected by Smith Travel Research (STR), an independent company, and made available in the form of STR reports. To calculate RevPar, multiply a hotel's daily average room rate by its occupancy rate. If a hotel's average room rate today is $95 and the occupancy rate is 80 percent, then the RevPar is $76.

The graph on the next page illustrates the percentage of TMI's 200 hotels that beat the RevPar of their competitors on a yearly basis. With Gary at the helm as TMI's CEO, the performance of the hotels he gave to his employees via the ESOP was outstanding from the start. Then that performance improved by 15 percent from 74 percent in 1999 to 85 percent in 2006.

At the same time, the hotels that Gary owned as he built his second lodging empire performed at slightly higher levels since the average age was a bit lower. The average of the TMI portfolio was only 4.86 years—hardly approaching obsolescence. Gary built his properties to last 40 or 50 years. The hotels in Gary's portfolio were somewhat younger on average, but that was because he was adding more new properties. His portfolio contained hotels built in the 1980s and 1990s, too.

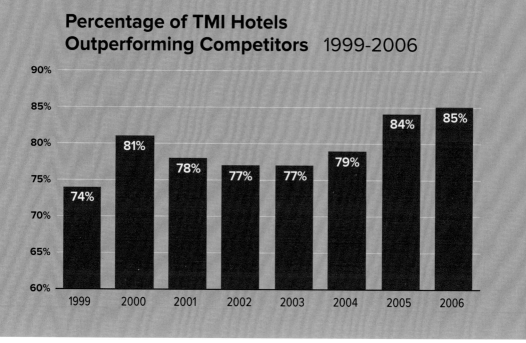

Percentage of TMI Hotels Outperforming Competitors 1999-2006

Year	Percentage
1999	74%
2000	81%
2001	78%
2002	77%
2003	77%
2004	79%
2005	84%
2006	85%

That the TMI hotels were in no way a risky proposition, as the Hans suit alleged, was further disproven by their EBITDA record. EBITDA is an acronym (albeit a bit of a tongue twister) for earnings before interest, taxes, depreciation and amortization. To calculate EBITDA, add net (not gross) profit to interest, taxes, depreciation and amortization. This is used as an indicator of a company's earning potential and used to compare profitability between companies and industries since EBITDA disregards financing issues and accounting methods.

In the graph on the opposite page, TMI's total revenue and EBITDA amounts are listed for 2000 through 2006. The EBITDA margin for TMI was impressive, ranging from 34 to 39 percent through this period. The EBITDA margin measures a company's operating profitability as a percentage of total revenue. To calculate, simply divide EBITDA by revenue. Both the EBITDA and EBITDA margins were consistently at least 15 percent above those of competitors.

Given Gary's long record of success in the lodging industry, there was no reason to suspect that suddenly TMI's hotels would perform poorly—especially with Gary continuing to run the company. The original amount asked

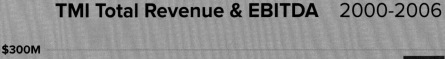

TMI Total Revenue & EBITDA   2000-2006

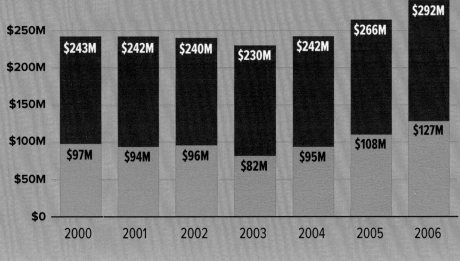

for in Hans suit was more than $200 million—a staggering sum plucked from the litigious ether. But what if that hyperbole became a sledgehammer in the delirium of legal proceedings? That scepter weighed heavily on Gary, which was the point—aimed at effecting an out-of-court settlement for a sizable prize. Such are the raiders of the golden pot.

But that was a severe misjudgment of character. Gary was prepared to fight.

In the immediate future, Gary was faced with spending considerable time defending himself and with spending millions of dollars in legal fees. His time and money would have otherwise been put to use productively building hotels and creating jobs.

"It wasn't fun having that lawsuit around our necks," Dobmeier recalled.

Worst of all for TMI was that Gary was forced to resign from leading the company. Since he had no intention of settling, he needed to break from TMI so that the statute of limitations on the lawsuit would begin running. Otherwise, however Hans would be resolved, the litigants could still sue for something related to the original suit.

CHAPTER ELEVEN

Cashing Out

Industry is fortune's right hand
and frugality her left.

John Ray

IN FEBRUARY 2005, Warren de Haan received a phone call from Kurt Altvater, a senior loan originator at Countrywide, saying that "there's a guy who owns between 300 and 400 hotels who wants to borrow $125 million." A year before, de Haan had co-founded Countrywide Financial Corporation's (CFC) commercial real estate finance business. This division at CFC soon became one of the largest lending platforms in the U.S., with commercial real estate loans totaling billions of dollars per year. Between 10 and 20 percent of these loans every year were for hotel properties. CFC became the nation's largest mortgager overall before the Great Recession hit in 2008.

De Haan was deeply puzzled. "How is it I've never heard about Gary Tharaldson?" he asked. De Haan had earned a B.S. degree from the Cornell School of Hotel Administration and also graduated from Hotel Institute Montreux, Switzerland. As a banker, de Haan had worked on financing many of the prominent hotel investors in the U.S. "Surely," he thought, "I should have heard about this guy." But as fast as Gary was flying in the hospitality industry, he was also flying under the financial industry's radar. Gary was still using local and regional banks for his deals. CFC was located in Calabasas, California, a small city nestled in the Santa Monica Mountains on the northwest border of the City of Los Angeles.

De Haan was also suspicious about the fact that Gary wanted to close in 21 days, which was a very short period to originate such large refinancing. Twenty-five of Gary's hotels were involved, which would require significant due diligence on de Haan's part to assess their value and performance.

De Haan called banking associates who told him about Gary. Still, de Haan was incredulous and called Gary in Las Vegas. De Haan was won over quickly by Gary's direct, open manner. Soon after the conversation, Gary sent him the documentation, which clearly demonstrated the breadth of his lodging holdings and their financial strength.

Gary wanted to refinance the hotels to take advantage of the recent 5 percent interest rates. "Hell, I've never seen interest rates this low," he told de Haan. This would decrease his debt service by over $2.5 million per year.

Given the health of Gary's finances, de Haan offered to increase the amount of the loan.

"I want to keep my assets long term and don't want to leverage them more than 65 percent," Gary responded. The $125 million constituted 65 percent of the hotels' worth, which is considered conservative leverage in the financial industry—and in keeping with Gary's fiscal strategy.

———————

In the afternoon on the day before Thanksgiving 2005, Gary called de Haan directly. "I want to borrow another $140 million," he said. "Can we do that?"

"Of course we can do that," de Haan replied immediately.

Gary then asked if de Haan could lock in the interest rate for the loan. The Treasury rate (or Treasury yield,

Warren de Haan was a key player in Archon deal and in resolving several of Gary's financial challenges.

———————

the interest rate for loans to the U.S. government) had declined again but could easily recover before business resumed after the holiday.

"Gary's hotels were good assets," de Haan said later. As well, he trusted Gary after their first deal and locked down the interest rate within 15 minutes of ending the call.

"Gary didn't push for every single basis point in the interest rate," de Haan remarked, "because he knew that locking in the Treasury was the single most important thing he could do going into Thanksgiving weekend. And I knew that he would figure out which hotels to put in the refinancing pool later."

In September 2005, Gary called de Haan and asked him to set up the financing to buy the Westward Ho Hotel and Casino on the Las Vegas Strip. Gary and Centex Destination Properties had an opportunity to buy the casino for $145.5 million, as mentioned in the opening chapter.

"I know it's a weird loan," Gary said, "but what can you do for me?"

As de Haan recalled, "It was not a normal deal for us, because we were making long-term, fixed-rate loans, and Gary needed a shorter-term loan." Still, de Haan and his team went to bat for Gary and met with CFC's president and COO. "We weren't in the business of making bridge loans, especially on buildings about to be demolished in Las Vegas on the Strip with no cash flow."

Centex was planning a huge casino and resort development to replace the Westward Ho, complete with a 600-foot-high giant Ferris wheel. This would have been 50 feet higher than the current world's tallest Ferris wheel, which was built in Las Vegas in 2014.

De Haan was to provide the financing Gary wanted at attractive rates because he knew Gary would pay it back. He was able to convey this conviction to his bosses and persuade CFC to make the unusual loan.

When the loan closed, de Haan and Altvater flew to Las Vegas to meet Gary and his wife, Connie, for a celebratory dinner at Fleming's Prime Steakhouse & Wine Bar.

"We're seeing hotel buyers starting to pay very attractive prices for hotels now," Warren told Gary during the meal. "And there are a number of big opportunity funds that are looking in the hotel sector for big portfolios. Have you ever considered selling your company?"

"That's interesting, Warren," Gary replied, "but I wouldn't know what to do with my time or my money if I sold the hotels."

"Fair enough," de Haan said. He enjoyed the rest of the evening and flew back to Calabasas.

As de Haan predicted, Gary paid the loan back and did so quickly. In fact, this was the deal where Gary ended up making $108 million the following September, when Harrah's Entertainment bought the Westward Ho from him.

Two months after the dinner at Fleming's, in November 2005, Gary called de Haan. "Warren, I need you to come to Las Vegas to see me," Gary said. "Something big has come up and we need to talk."

De Haan left CFC headquarters right away and flew to Las Vegas, where he learned that Archon Hospitality LP had just offered more than $2 billion for all the hotels in TMI's and in Gary's portfolios. This would constitute the largest sale in the history of the hospitality industry by far. Archon is a resort and hotel management company that is a subsidiary of the Goldman Sachs Group, Inc.

As TMI's trustee, Gary had the authority to sell the company's hotels—which was the endgame. The strategic objective had always been to build up TMI's equity and sell the company so the employees would all be able to cash out. There was no rush to sell at this point, but the offer was too good to ignore. In fact, Archon was valuing the hotels in both portfolios at a third higher than Gary's assessment.

Gary asked de Haan to assess the deal. De Haan replied, "Look, Gary, I'm not an expert investment banker, I'm not in the investment sales business. It's not what I do."

"But Warren, I need you to deal with these guys," Gary said.

Gary, as Warren was learning, is very loyal to the people he does business with. The two men had established considerable trust. "He knew that I would always look out for his and his family's best interests," de Haan later said. "Secondly, I knew well how to deal with guys on Wall Street and Gary was not a big fan of those types."

De Haan reviewed the Archon proposal, "which was convoluted to say the least," he recalled. For the next three weeks, he and Gary talked through the offer's complexities and what they meant for Gary and TMI.

"Look, Gary," de Haan said when they completed their assessment, "I can definitely be helpful with the family assets. I can negotiate on your behalf for the asset sale and protect your interests. And I can speak the same language as the Archon guys to help them understand they need to pay more, and they're still going to get a fair deal."

However, de Haan felt uneasy about representing TMI's interests. "I am not comfortable with the nuances and implications of an asset sale for an ESOP," he told Gary. As well, the ESOP still had the Hans lawsuit to resolve.

As a result, Gary and de Haan interviewed several of the major investment banks and ultimately chose Morgan Stanley to be the lead advisor on the sale of the ESOP assets.

In mid-December 2005, several members of the Archon team—headed by Todd Giannoble, Archon's president—visited Gary in Fargo as part of their due diligence regarding the deal. They wanted to meet Gary in person, along with TMI's top people, at their headquarters in Fargo. The same executives, including Dobmeier and Larson, also ran Gary's hotels and headed the development of new properties.

The Archon executives flew from their headquarters in Irving, Texas, to Minneapolis and then drove 240 miles to Fargo in a black limousine.

Gary and de Haan were still negotiating the terms of the purchase agreement and a letter of intent had yet to be signed. This first meeting was important to the negotiations as both sides assessed each other. De Haan later characterized the Archon team as "very smart, very seasoned. They were good but very tough negotiators."

The Archon team arrived in their limo just as Gary pulled up in a dull gold-colored 2001 Taurus. The Archon team was astounded and later that day said to de Haan, "This guy has built almost 400 hotels and that's the car he drives? Are you serious?"

De Haan laughed because that was just the beginning of their introduction to Gary's world. For lunch, Gary took them to his favorite restaurant, Red Lobster, where he often eats dessert before the main course—or at least, he did at the time. Since then, his favorite pastry, key lime pie, has been taken off Red Lobster's menu. This restaurant, or any chain eatery, was definitely not where Archon executives would take a client to lunch.

Despite the gastronomic mismatch, Giannoble and the other Archon officials were deeply impressed by Gary's knowledge of the hotel business, especially the two sectors he was dominating, limited-service and extended-stay. They were also amazed that they could ask questions about particular hotels and Gary responded with exact numbers regarding occupancy, ADR, EBITDA and so on.

The afternoon meetings went well, and the Archon team ended the day with a very positive view of TMI and the top executives they met.

To celebrate, Gary took the team and de Haan out for fine dining—at the local Holiday Inn.

"I remember Giannoble looking at the menu, and he's a wine connoisseur," de Haan said. "The most expensive bottle of wine was $12. He goes, 'I'm not sure if I can even order this wine.'"

Although not intended on Gary's part, the entire day involved a brilliant juxtaposition between Gary's down-home, straightforward approach to business and life, and the aggressive, sophisticated *élan de l'âme* typical of

New York financial giants. This contrast kept the Archon team off balance, and they would not regain balance, let alone the upper hand, throughout the negotiations.

In late January 2006, Gary underwent double knee replacement surgery at St. Rose Dominican's Joint Replacement Center in Henderson, Nevada. The surgery became necessary mostly as the result of Gary's devotion to softball. Since he founded Tharaldson Insurance Agency in the early 1970s, Gary has always fielded a team that he played on, coached and sponsored. He provided uniforms and transportation, lodging and meals for his players, many of whom also worked for him. Gary played in hundreds of tournaments and more than 3,000 games. Pitching, batting, catching, running bases, let alone practices and pickup games, all added up to tremendous, repetitive wear on Gary's knees.

Throughout his career, Gary was so passionate about softball that often it seemed building hotels was his hobby and winning on the diamond was his job. The tournament Gary's teams played in most often was the annual Sam McQuade, Sr./Budweiser Charity Softball Tournament (known as, "the McQuade"), which is held in Bismarck on the third weekend in June. The McQuade is the largest—and the most competitive—nonprofit, slow-pitch softball tournament held on a single weekend in the U.S. The tournament was founded in 1976 by the owner of McQuade Distributing Company, which distributes Budweiser beers in the Bismarck area. The first tournament attracted 103 teams, competing in four divisions. Currently, the McQuade brings more than 450 teams from across the country and from Manitoba and Saskatchewan to compete in 10 men's and five women's divisions.

Several years after Dobmeier started working for Gary in 1984, Gary asked him to play on the softball team at the McQuade, since one of his players was unavailable that weekend. Although Dobmeier has not played much softball, he had played on his college baseball team. No doubt he would have made the transition to the bigger-ball, slow-pitch sport with ease.

At a critical point in one of the games that weekend, the bases were loaded and Dobmeier was at bat. He swung and popped up the ball for an easy out and the end of the inning.

"When I came back to the dugout, Gary chewed me out," Dobmeier

Softball trophies won by the Tharaldson Insurance team on display at the Labor Club in Valley City, ND.

recalled. "We had a lot in common—we loved athletics and loved to win. I'm a competitor, too."

Even so, Dobmeier responded to getting chewed out by saying, "Hey, this isn't work, this is supposed to be fun." Later, Dobmeier told Gary he would run his hotels and do his best to make him successful, but he wouldn't play softball with him again. "In business, I always looked at Gary as the financial driver, the financial genius, and I thought I was pretty good at developing systems and implementing what Gary wanted."

They played basketball together after that weekend, which Gary also loved and played on various teams into his 40s. But he wasn't as fiercely competitive on the court as on the diamond.

As Matthew 6:24 puts it, you can't serve two masters—even if they are in the same person (and dugout).

Gary has been inducted into three Halls of Fame: the North Dakota Softball Hall of Fame, as a player, in 1995; the American Softball Associ-

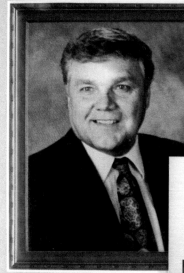

1995
N.D.A.S.A. HALL OF FAME
GARY THARALDSON
FARGO, NORTH DAKOTA

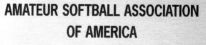

AMATEUR SOFTBALL ASSOCIATION
OF AMERICA

Hall of Fame

Gary Tharaldson
2011
FARGO, NORTH DAKOTA
SPONSOR

In recognition of outstanding ability as demonstrated in softball competition, sportsmanship, integrity, character, and contribution to the sport of softball this citation bears witness that his name shall forever be in the AMATEUR SOFTBALL ASSOCIATION HALL OF FAME.

Gary has dedicated much of his life to supporting ASA Softball as a sponsor for not just one or two divisions but across the whole spectrum of ASA Softball. He was a sponsor for 38 years of the Men's A, B and C Slow Pitch Divisions and supported five different levels of senior ball for a total of 24 years. Gary sponsored Women's teams for 15 years as well as both Boys and Girls Junior Olympic Teams. His sponsored teams have participated in over 30 National Tournaments. Outside of his teams, Gary gave back by providing North Dakota state tournament trophies and banners for all divisions for 12 years and has sponsored the North Dakota Hall of Fame Banquet for 10 years. Gary has been a key component in keeping the upper division of the McQuade Charity Tournament going. Gary was also a player during his time as sponsor winning two National Championships and over 1,000 games as a pitcher.

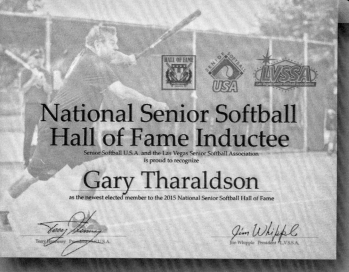

National Senior Softball
Hall of Fame Inductee

Senior Softball U.S.A. and the Las Vegas Senior Softball Association
is proud to recognize

Gary Tharaldson

as the newest elected member to the 2015 National Senior Softball Hall of Fame

Terry Hennessy, President S.S.U.S.A.

Jim Whipple, President LVSSA

Gary Tharaldson's Softball Rings (left to right):

1 Las Vegas Senior Softball Association World Championship
2 Softball Players Association World Championship
3 Softball Players Association World Championship
4 National Senior Softball Hall of Fame
5 Softball Players Association World Championship
6 Softball Players Association World Championship
7 Senior Softball USA World Championship
8 Amateur Softball Association
9 Senior Softball USA Winter World Championship
10 Senior Softball USA World Championship
11 Las Vegas Senior Softball Association World Championship
12 North Dakota Amateur Softball Association
13 Las Vegas Senior Softball Association World Championship

Gary has been inducted into three Halls of Fame: the North Dakota
Softball Hall of Fame, as a player, in 1995; the American Softball
Association Hall of Fame, as a sponsor, in 2011; and the National
Senior Softball Hall of Fame in 2015, as a manager.

Family vacation in Jamaica in 2015. Left to right, Gary II, Grant, Gary, Connie, Dani, Bobbi.

ation Hall of Fame, as a sponsor, in 2011; and the National Senior Softball Hall of Fame in 2015, as a manager.

In the National Senior Softball Hall of Fame's newsletter announcing the "Class of 2015," Russ Curtis, who played for Tharaldson Enterprises in Las Vegas, wrote:

> In the past 15 years, Gary has amassed a very impressive resume as a manager. His teams have captured 19 world championships and were runners-up 11 times. … Gary has a unique feel for the game of softball, both as a player and a manager. Strategy plays a big part in how he manages. He always seems to know just the right time to make a pitching change or when to use a pinch hitter in a key situation. Gary is a team-first manager who doesn't play favorites. When you play for Gary, you know what your role is and who's in charge!

Curtis maintained a batting average of .800 and was inducted into the National Senior Softball Hall of Fame as a player in 2008. Although Gary doesn't classify himself as an elite player, he pitched in more than 1,000 games and maintained a .500 batting average, as noted in 2011 when he was inducted into the American Softball Association Hall of Fame. The North

Dakota State Amateur Softball Association's newsletter also reported that "[h]e competed successfully at all levels of ASA play from Class A, B and C through all levels of masters and seniors play. His teams won state championships 20 times, won regional titles 6 times.... A measure of his athletic ability can be judged by the fact that he was still competing as a pitcher on a Class A slow pitch team at the age of 49."

Gary's sponsorship of softball in North Dakota and Las Vegas included men's, women's and coed teams at all adult levels. He also sponsored boys and girls teams in the Junior Olympics softball program and girls teams in the Junior Olympics fast pitch program. As well, Gary sponsored Little League and Babe Ruth baseball teams. Not only did Gary provide uniforms, equipment, entry fees and travel and accommodation, he donated the money to build a softball diamond in Valley City and a baseball complex in Fargo.

For Gary, "softball is the only thing I do that's not business or family-oriented. I do it for myself. I like the challenge of the game. Softball has allowed me to try to be the best I could be at a sport. I was fortunate to be on some very good teams, and I was not the best player. I always batted in the bottom of the order, but I competed in my own way and I think I was a good leader."

But softball doesn't take away from family or business. "I always have a lot of balls in the air at one time," Gary said. "In business, I have a lot going on and the same in my personal life. I also attend over a hundred games a year that my kids play in." Gary spends evenings and weekends with his wife and children at home and at their lake house. There are also regular family vacations, including spending Christmas in Hawaii every year at a timeshare resort. Gary and Connie also took their children to London and Paris in 2015, for example.

Perhaps this ability to juggle has something to do with Gary's Norwegian heritage. According to Tor Dahl, a business consultant and associate professor in public health at the University of Minnesota, "Norwegians make up for days away from work by what is called *skippertak*. It means that you work like an absolute maniac when you have to work … You can get an incredible amount of stuff done in a very short period of time." Dahl founded Dahl & Associates, which bills itself as a "pioneer and leader in productivity improvement."

While Gary was not an absolute maniac, he followed the 25/40 rule, spending less time in the office than most entrepreneurs, but more time outside the office thinking about how to improve his business.

Gary's knees, however, were not as Norwegian as the rest of him. They started wearing out from all the *skippertak* on the diamond until Gary finally went to be examined at Crovetti Orthopaedics and Sports Medicine in Henderson in the fall of 2005. Gary underwent double knee replacement surgery in late January 2006, as mentioned earlier.

Throughout January and February 2006, de Haan continued to take the lead in negotiating, primarily with Todd Giannoble, Archon's president. Gary was recovering from surgery and weaning himself off painkillers as quickly as possible so he could complete the deal with a clear mind.

A letter of intent to sell/purchase 143 hotels for $1.35 billion was signed by both parties. Meanwhile, the TMI hotel deal was being negotiated separately.

In mid-March, less than two weeks before the sale of Gary's hotels was scheduled to close, Giannoble called de Haan and said, "I want to come see you and Gary in Vegas."

Gary and de Haan knew exactly what this was about. Throughout the negotiations, de Haan held fast about the sale price. Giannoble found this very frustrating and decided to try one last time in person. "People like Giannoble buy assets strategically for a living," Gary explained. "They are trying to get the best returns for their investors. To the extent that assets are not exactly as they had seen them at the outset, they negotiate to reprice the deal."

After the letter of intent was signed, Giannoble's team examined Gary's hotels and his company in depth. For example, there were concerns about the benefits plan for Gary's employees. The buyer would be required to increase the plan's benefits, which would decrease cash flow going forward.

"At this point in the transaction, the biggest part of my job was staving off the retrade," de Haan recalled. "They started at about $180 million in price reductions." While de Haan's manner throughout negotiations was to remain calm, Giannoble was more inclined to spark heated discussions. Still, both de Haan and Gary developed considerable respect for Giannoble who was very good at his job, in their estimation. "If I was on the other side, I would also be tough," de Haan said. "I would try to get every price reduction I could."

Leverage, however, belonged to Gary. "Giannoble was under a lot of pressure to get this deal done," de Haan related. "By this time, he had spent

Gary Tharaldson

inducted into

THE SCANDINAVIAN-AMERICAN HALL OF FAME

MINOT, NORTH DAKOTA, USA

October 8, 2003

Chances are good you've experienced Gary Tharaldson's hospitality when traveling the United States. He is founder, owner, and president of Tharaldson Companies, which builds and operates hotels and motels across the country. Tharaldson Property Management, Inc., the nation's largest independent hotel property management company, operates 350 inns in 35 states, and at any given time Tharaldson Development Company has 20 to 30 more sites planned or under construction. The majority of Tharaldson properties are franchisees of Marriott, Choice Hotels, and Hilton.

After brief careers in teaching and insurance the Dazey, North Dakota native and Norwegian-American entered the business in 1982 with the purchase of a Super 8 motel in Valley City, ND. In just 10 years, Tharaldson's company grew into the nation's largest hotel developer with an innovative, unique-to-the-industry approach: think *small*. Rather than chasing success in major lodging markets, Tharaldson built in cities with populations of under 100,000—often college towns in the Midwest—and opted for inns with fewer rooms than the industry standard. The idea was to reduce costs, keep occupancy high, and reap higher profits.

Tharaldson believes location is key, and while he delegates much responsibility in his company to others, he reserves for himself the thrill of the hunt for new property sites. The company recently began focusing on larger markets, where demand for hotel rooms continues to exceed supply. His success earned him a place on *Forbes* magazine's list of the 400 richest people in America. And he has shared his wealth by adopting an employee stock ownership program through which his associates own 50 percent of the company.

As well known as Gary Tharaldson is in the hotel industry, in North Dakota he is perhaps better known for his passion for slowpitch softball. In that realm also he has met with success, sponsoring and/or pitching on teams that have won numerous state, regional, and national titles. And how many softball teams fly to tournaments on a private jet?!

Gary Tharaldson was an 2003 inductee into the Scandinavian-American Hall of Fame during the Norsk Høstfest in Minot, ND. Høstfest is held annually each fall and has grown to become the largest Scandinavian festival in North America.

millions of dollars on legal due diligence, on consultants, on third-party appraisal reports and on lender deposits. If the transaction didn't happen, that would have made him look terrible internally."

The problem for Giannoble was that as attractive as this deal was, it was also unusual. He was not dealing with a big brokerage firm or an institutional seller. He was negotiating with an individual owner who held the ultimate advantage: He did not have to sell.

At the time, this deal involved the largest number of hotel assets ever included in a sale in the U.S.

The meeting in Gary's office ended with de Haan reiterating, "Look, we are not going to cave. You can either buy the hotels or not. It's your choice."

The one concession that Gary made was to reduce the sale price by $8 million. Also, three hotels were taken out of the deal since Gary didn't own the land but was leasing it. This reduced the sale price by another $26 million to $1.309 billion.

To conclude the deal, Gary was scheduled to sign all the documents in the midtown Manhattan offices of Sullivan & Cromwell LLP—the legal firm that often handles Goldman Sachs (Archon's parent company) transactions—on March 31.

De Haan booked rooms for himself and for Gary and Connie at the New York Palace on Madison Avenue between East 50th and East 51st Streets, right behind St. Patrick's Cathedral, and only three blocks from Sullivan & Cromwell.

"How much are the rooms at that hotel?" Gary asked de Haan when he called about finalizing arrangements a few days before flying to New York.

"It's about $600 a night," de Haan replied.

"That's too much," Gary said.

"Gary, you are about to close a $1.3 billion deal," de Haan said. "You should be staying at the Palace Hotel."

"No, no, no, I don't need to spend the extra money," Gary replied. "I'll get back to you."

De Haan couldn't help but laugh after Gary hung up. It was astounding and yet so typical of him to worry about such a minor expense in that context.

Meanwhile, Gary booked a room at the New York Marriott East Side, three and a half blocks from the Palace and farther from Sullivan & Cromwell.

Friday, March 31, was a sunny, breezy day with temperatures about 63 degrees F as Gary and Connie walked out of the Marriott onto Lexington Avenue at 8:30 a.m. Actually, only Connie was walking. Gary was still recovering from double knee surgery and was in a wheelchair. Six and a half blocks to the Sullivan & Cromwell's offices did not seem far. Gary and Connie decided to go on foot with Connie pushing the wheelchair. Not only were they twice as far away than they would have been if they had stayed at the Palace, but they had to negotiate more than twice as many curbs and street crossings.

By the time Gary and Connie crossed Park Avenue at East 49th Street, the wheelchair was malfunctioning. Although most sidewalk curbs in Manhattan slope down to the street, there is a fractured network of cracks in the asphalt surfaces, some deep enough to turn a pedestrian's ankle. The constant pounding of taxicabs, trucks and cars on the city's streets, along with the impact of ice, snow and rain, necessitate frequent piecemeal street repairs that create a dangerous topography for anyone with ambulatory challenges.

So, there were Gary and Connie trying to keep the wheels from falling off the wheelchair as they struggled past the Palace on their way north on Madison Avenue. No observer would surmise that this couple was on the way to close a $1.3 billion deal. Nor did Gary and Connie have the luxury of appreciating what remains of architecture in a city that is increasingly dominated by vertical monstrosities in every box shape unimaginatively imaginable. The historic part of the Palace faces Madison Avenue. It is a four-story brownstone structure that was originally built in 1882 as the Villard Houses, which were six private residences around a courtyard in the neo-Italian Renaissance style after the Palazzo della Cancelleria in Rome.

Neither Rome nor Renaissance elegance was on the Tharaldsons' minds, however. Instead, the challenge was crossing East 51st Street without getting run over by the horde of charging taxis seemingly driven by madmen. To the uninitiated, traffic laws in Manhattan would seem to be no more than driving tips adhered to strictly on the second Tuesday of every week. The same contest between the hobbled and the harried played on at the next three intersections.

Finally, Gary, Connie and the broken wheelchair arrived at the offices of Sullivan & Cromwell in a glass and steel high-rise office building on the northeast corner of Madison Avenue and East 54th Street. The building was constructed in 1981, just as Gary was about to begin his hotel development journey.

In the firm's meeting room, there were about 60 people, including de Haan and Jim Thompson, CFC's general counsel (and de Haan's partner at CFC who played a major role in the sale's success), and Gary's legal team from Skadden, Arps, Slate, Meagher & Flom LLP, headed by Rand April. Skadden is perennially ranked as the top Wall Street law firm. Also present were the Sullivan & Cromwell legal team, almost a dozen escrow officers and teams from the two lenders: Credit Suisse First Boston and Barclays Bank.

Four hours later, at 1 p.m., it became clear that the pace of completing and signing the hundreds of documents by all the parties present was slower than expected. Each hotel was a separate entity with a pile of documents to peruse for the last time and then sign. As well, once the deal closed, the funds were going to be wired to dozens of banks across the country, which was causing confusion. Gary and Connie could stay until midnight if necessary to get all the paperwork. But if the funds weren't wired by 5 p.m., they wouldn't go out until Monday, which would cost Gary $200,000 in interest. For the man who refused to book a $600 hotel room, this was not a pleasing scenario.

De Haan recalled several heated discussions since there didn't seem to be any leadership among the escrow officers who would make the wire transfers. Finally, Thompson, his partner at CFC, grabbed a piece of paper and took Gary aside to draw a map showing exactly where funds were to be wired. This brought instant clarity to the scenario and, minutes after the last documents were signed, the transfer were made—just in time.

Because of entitlement issues with 10 of the hotels, the sale of these properties was delayed until September. For simplicity's sake, the funds from this sale are included here. In total, $1.309 billion was transferred to dozens of accounts, per Gary's instructions. The entire outstanding debt of $452 million on the 140 hotels was paid off, which involved wire transfers to more than 50 banks. The closing fees cost Gary $17 million, and $15 million was set aside for repairs and maintenance for the hotels.

The remaining $825 million was wired to accounts involving various investment land deals Gary was working and to Gary's bank accounts. Also, $90 million was set aside to pay the estimated tax liability on the Archon sale.

As de Haan exhaled at day's end, he felt pleased with the outcome. "I helped get the highest price possible for Gary and his family with the best structure to protect them," he said.

Immediately after the deal closed, Gary and Connie took a cab to LaGuardia Airport and flew to Indianapolis, Indiana, to enjoy Final Four weekend of the National Collegiate Athletic Association's annual basketball tournament. The tournament is known as March Madness, which was also an apt appellation for Gary and Connie's experience completing the Archon sale.

Lost, Found & Legacy

2006-Present

CHAPTER TWELVE

The Year of Living Magically

The eye sees only what the mind
is prepared to comprehend.

Robertson Davies

HEDGEHOG OR HODGEPODGE? Gary didn't realize this was the question facing him as he sold his hotels in 2006. Gary's immediate challenge—that 99.99999 percent of the world's population can only dream about in the remotest way—was, what to do with $735,000,000 in cash?

However, operating in that magnitude has nothing to do with how ordinary people deal with money. It's not about paying off personal credit cards or student loan debts, or buying that house or car one has always wanted. Large amounts of money are really about taking responsibility for many people's lives and futures. Developing businesses provides jobs and careers, services and products for large numbers of people nationwide who in turn provide for their families, raise children and eventually send them to college so they can provide for their future and families. The more successful entrepreneurs are, the heavier their responsibilities become. Wealth creation is a job and a discipline far more than the means to indulgence.

As soon as the Archon deal was completed (in two parts: 130 hotels sold in March and 10 hotels sold in September 2006), the tax clock started ticking. According to the Internal Revenue Code, when there is a financial gain from the sale of a business or investment property, there is also a tax to pay. However, the Code allows for an exception, articulated in Section 1031, allowing capital gains tax to be deferred if the proceeds are reinvested "in similar property as part of a qualifying like-kind exchange."

Since Gary's hotels are investment properties, he was allowed to take as much of the $735 million as he wanted and reinvest in other properties. In this case, "like-kind" applied to any real estate except for personal use. Gary wasn't able to defer capital gains by purchasing a vacation home, for example.

Importantly, according to the Code, Gary had only 45 days to identify properties and 180 days to close on those properties. That was not so easy to do, well and wisely, with so much money to spend.

The timing of the Archon deal allowed Gary to have $170 million wired immediately to buy the Westward Ho from his partner, Centex Destination Properties. This amount included paying off the debt for the original $145.5 million purchase price a year ago, $10 million in profit to Centex, $12 million for demolition costs and $3 million to the equity holders (including interest). As outlined in Chapter Zero, Gary sold the Westward Ho six months later, in September 2006, and made $108 million in profits. These profits, in turn, were invested via 1031 in CityView, a 38-acre property in Las Vegas. The site is on Dean Martin Drive, which runs parallel to I-15. The property was (and remains) a business park, but it is zoned for casinos and resorts and sits less than a mile from the busiest part of the Strip at the corner of Flamingo Road. Gary invested almost $100 million in CityView via 1031 as soon as the Archon deal closed. The additional investment from the Westward Ho sale allowed him to own the property outright.

Once the $170 million was wired for the Westward Ho deal, Gary had $565 million available for 1031 exchanges and other investments. "Gary likes to have his money invested," said Joe Blagg in an interview. Blagg, who began working for Gary in 2006, is his development and finance manager. "He doesn't like cash sitting in a bank." The reason is obvious: The return on bank deposits is minimal, often less than inflation, while Gary's investments were averaging a 10 percent return per year.

One big difference between CityView and Gary's past investments was that the hotels had much greater liquidity than land intended for commercial, retail or residential development.

"The fox knows many things, but the hedgehog knows one big thing." Isaiah Berlin wrote in *The Hedgehog and the Fox* (1993), as cited in *Good to Great: Why Some Companies Make the Leap and Others Don't* by business consultant and author Jim Collins. Collins goes on to write:

Berlin extrapolated from this little parable to divide people into two basic groups: foxes and hedgehogs. Foxes pursue many ends at the same time and see the world in all its complexity. They are "scattered or diffused, moving on many levels," says Berlin, never integrating their thinking into one overall concept or unifying vision. Hedgehogs, on the other hand, simplify a complex world into a single organizing idea, or a basic principle or concept that unifies and guides everything.

It's hedgehogs who make the biggest impact on the world—for example, Einstein. "What could be more simple than e = mc²?" Collins asks. Then he illustrates how Walgreens, for example, succeeds "so brilliantly by taking one simple concept and just doing it with excellence and imagination." In contrast, other companies act like foxes "in hodgepodge fashion, with no obvious unifying theme."

According to Collins, a company's "Hedgehog Concept is a simple crystal-line concept that flows from deep understanding about the intersection of the following three circles:

1. What you can be the best in the world at (and, equally important, what you cannot be best in the world at).

2. What drives your economic engine? All the good-to-great companies … discovered the single denominator—profit per x—that had the greatest impact on their economics.

3. What you are deeply passionate about. The good-to-great companies focused on those activities that ignited their passion."

The book was published in 2001 and Gary read it. But his company had already gone from good to great. The book confirmed how Gary was already operating. He had discovered his passion in the early 1980s, he was certainly building hotels in his sector—limited-service and extended-stay—better than anyone else, and he understood from the start how profits drove the Tharaldson economic engine. More than any other hotel developer, Gary focused his energies on figuring out, via innovations and efficiencies, how to run the most profitable hotel company per dollar of revenue in the country. In fact, Gary has stated—for example, on KFYR radio during an interview by

Scott Hennen on September 9, 2017—that his company might be the most profitable in any economic sector per dollar revenue.

Stated differently, Gary's insight into what drove his success financially was profit per hotel. This clear perception was applied at all phases from building costs and procurement to labor costs and high service standards. Occupancy rates were kept high and costs low, as a result.

Gary's mantra, "Keep it simple," guided him and his companies with hedgehog focus and determination. However, the only component in Collins' analysis that Gary had yet to integrate was understanding what he cannot be best in the world at. This would soon stampede through his business and personal life.

As a hedgehog, Gary had a clear strategic plan that worked extremely well. As discussed in Chapter Five, the exit plan is a crucial component of strategic thinking. Col. Warden defines the exit plan as "transition[ing] effectively from success or failure with finesse." Selling the hotels marked the end of Gary's strategic plan to build his second lodging empire.

Complicating the exit plan were the deadlines the IRS imposes on 1031 exchanges, mentioned above. The timing of this pressure could not have been worse. As Gary recovered from double knee replacement surgery, his back pain worsened. For years, he hadn't been able to sleep on his left side. In February 2006, Gary had X-rays taken that revealed a cracked vertebra. The only injury Gary had sustained that could have hurt his back was in a car accident in Brooklyn Center, Minnesota, in 1988.

On April 12, 2006, less than two weeks after closing the Archon deal, Gary underwent surgery again. The crushed vertebra was removed, and the vertebrae immediately above and below were fused together. A small metal plate was inserted to support his healing spine, and Gary was put in a body cast for six weeks.

"Normally we don't do surgeries this close," Gary's doctor said. "But I think you're pretty strong and we can do it. You will be able to handle it physically. The thing is, sometimes it's a lot harder on people mentally."

That was Gary's experience. "I remember getting sad during that time.

Connie was always really good through it all, and I remember getting irritable at the kids sometimes, too," Gary recalled with obvious regret.

Also, Gary was back on painkillers again at the same time as he was investing such a large amount of money. As much as he tried to limit his intake of hydrocodone, he wasn't able to taper off the narcotic until December.

Hydrocodone's side effects include anxiety, depression, fatigue, and less commonly agitation and altered mood. "When I was in pain, I didn't want to do anything," Gary recalled. "Then after I took a pill, I felt great and that I could do anything. The drugs fluctuated my mind so when everything was great, I really wanted to do a deal. I'm a deal junkie anyway."

There were times when Gary told employees involved in development and other investments, not to bring him deals until he recovered. "Kyle came to see me in the hospital when I was practically incoherent," Gary said. "I remember getting upset." Kyle Newman started working for Gary helping out in the corporate office after finishing university in 2000.

Gary's problem was that the 1031 clock was ticking, and he was determined to take advantage of this provision rather than pay capital gains tax and sit on the remaining funds. Normally, Gary would have then focused on buying land to build hotels, but he had far too much money to invest. As well, he already owned enough prospective hotel sites for the near future.

Also, a real estate boom was at full throttle in 2006. The median price for a new home had more than doubled nationwide from $122,000 in 1992 to more than $244,000 in 2006. The hottest markets included the Las Vegas, Phoenix, Denver and Austin, Texas, areas. The boom included new retail and office space.

In addition to the $170 million 1031 exchange for the Westward Ho, Gary invested the remaining $565 million from the Archon sale in other 1031 exchanges (including $99.7 million towards owning CityView, as mentioned above).

These exchanges included seven tracts of land, totaling 4,024 acres, in Colorado. Almost all of this land was seen as prime locations for upscale single-family-unit housing developments. Sierra Ridge, for example, consists of 314 acres in Douglas County, whose northern border runs about five miles

Architect's rendering of part of Mahogany, a lakeside residential resort community, at Lake Travis, TX.

south of Denver's southern city limits. The county includes numerous suburbs and small cities and stretches south to within 10 miles of Colorado Springs. Douglas County enjoys the highest median household income of any county in the state and has been growing rapidly. The county's population almost tripled from 1980 to 1990 and then tripled again by 2000 to 175,766 residents. Over the next six years, the population grew by 70,000 people. The median price of a new home in Douglas county hit $323,103 at the beginning of 2007.

Sierra Ridge seemed like a sure bet to make a healthy return on the $26 million investment within a few years. The property was zoned for 950 single-family houses. Gary did not plan to build the houses but to sell the lots to a large home-building company.

Gary also invested $127.3 million via 1031 exchange in 1,053 acres of commercial and mixed-use properties in Texas, Georgia, Arizona and Las Vegas.

"A mixed-use property is often about half for single-family homes and the other half for multi-family dwellings, office buildings and retail outlets," Gary explained. For example, via 1031, Gary acquired 333 acres for mixed-use development in Manvel, Texas, near Houston.

Sites for commercial development only tended to be smaller, such as the five-acre lot for commercial development ($11.2 million) on the Las Vegas Strip about two miles south of the airport. Other smaller tracts included 14- and 15-acre commercial sites in Phoenix for a total of $12.6 million.

During 2006, in addition to 1031 exchanges, Gary bought various properties in Colorado, Texas and Las Vegas for $81.7 million with money he had accumulated from hotel profits and from the sale of various properties not part of the Archon deal. For $56.4 million, he acquired five properties to be developed as luxury residential resorts, including a dude ranch community in Colorado ski country, two lake resort communities in central Texas (including Mahogany, shown in the drawing on the opposite page), and a golf and ski community in the foothills of the San Juan Mountains in southern Colorado.

The commercial concept was to divide the land into lots at each location and then sell them to affluent clients for upscale second or vacation homes. In total, the five properties cover 1,826 acres of undeveloped land in stunningly beautiful settings.

Another avenue of investment for Gary's cash was making loans to construction projects and to speculators buying land, which totaled $255.9 million in 2006 and early 2007. For example, Gary loaned out $55.3 million for commercial, multi-use and multi-family projects in Arizona and Nevada. As well he lent out $60.6 million on single-family developments in California and Nevada.

The largest and most interesting loan Gary made was to a land speculator in Phoenix with a curious reputation—and the loan might have an even more curious outcome.

Among the dozens of local banks Gary dealt with when he needed construction loans was BNC National Bank, which has most of its branches in North Dakota. One of the loan officers who arranged about a dozen loans to Gary, mostly to construct hotels, was Brad Scott, who left BNC in 2005 to form his own company called Scott Financial Corporation (SFC).

Irrigated farmland in the Harquahala Valley, AZ.

"Then, of course, I became a big target for Scott after the Archon sale because he could make a lot of money for the stuff I was doing," Gary said. "I was trying to lend out money to projects that Scott was underwriting and putting together."

"Many people were swirling around Gary then," de Haan recalled. "Some had decent intent and others viewed him as just a way to make a bunch of dough." Gary had a habit of picking up his cell phone and listening whether or not he knew the person calling. Those with good intent urged Gary to screen his calls.

In the fall of 2006, Scott contacted Gary about a deal involving 15,000 acres of productive farmland in the Harquahala Valley, 70 miles west of Phoenix. Gary was intrigued and soon flew to Phoenix to meet Conley Wolfswinkel, the president of W Holdings LLC. Wolfswinkel is a land baron who owned 80,000 acres at the time in the Phoenix area. His company acquires properties to sell to commercial and residential developers.

Wolfswinkel wanted to borrow $30 million to replace existing loans from financial institutions on the 15,000 acres in Harquahala. He wanted to free up capital by lowering his debt service so he could buy more land elsewhere in the state. Gary found his offer to pay 14 percent interest per year very attractive. Gary returned to Las Vegas and wired the funds to Wolfswinkel.

"Who lends $30 million based on meeting some guy for a week?" de Haan asked rhetorically in an interview. "Not to undermine Conley in any way—I happen to be a big fan of his—but if you're a prudent investor, he's not attracting that kind of capital."

Wolfswinkel had become a legend in the Phoenix area. Five years younger than Gary, he was a leading land speculator in Arizona who, like Gary, started with nothing and became a very wealthy tycoon. Unlike Gary, he collected at least as many enemies as admirers, and was convicted in 1993, in the aftermath of the savings and loan (S&L) scandal, of floating bad checks. Wolfswinkel was fined more than $2 billion, which he settled for $21.4 million, and he was put on probation.

"Conley got in trouble because he borrowed from an S&L," Gary said. "His side of the story is that he had a relationship with the S&L such that he could borrow money and then sign the documents when he got back into town. So he signed the documents several days after the loan and they got him on some kind of fraud."

Wolfswinkel maintained that the U.S. Attorney's office passed on the case, but an overzealous FBI agent wanted to get him. After meeting Wolfswinkel in person, Gary was satisfied with his explanation and wasn't bothered by other legal issues, such as an ongoing lawsuit concerning a contested $74 million land deal, which was filed in 2003. The case involved the sale of 13,500 acres near Phoenix to W Holdings.

Gary made a judgment about the man based on intuition rather than assessing him solely on his blemished record. As well, Wolfswinkel had a history of attracting high-end investors and, despite travails, had always performed well for them.

Gary was not the only one who had confidence in Wolfswinkel despite his predicaments. Crocker Liu, PhD, held the McCord Chair at Arizona State University's W.P. Carey School of Business from 2006 to 2009. Liu played a "pivotal role in restoring Wolfswinkel's stature in the local business community," reported Jan Buchholz in Phoenix Business Journal in June 2008. The article quoted Liu saying "Conley was up front with me about his trials and tribulations, and I was up front with him because I'm that way. ... I'm in the education business. I teach people how to avoid the same mistakes over and over. I thought what better person to teach them than Conley, who was willing to talk up front about what he's faced, instead of others who go out of their way to hide their failures." At Liu's request, Wolfswinkel spoke at the ASU business school's first national real estate conference in February 2008.

When Gary met Wolfswinkel two years earlier, he was reemerging as one of the major land barons in Arizona. In the spring of 2007, Wolfswinkel contacted Gary about borrowing an additional $40 million to replace other loans on the Harquahala acreage. Wolfswinkel wanted to do more land speculating and offered Gary the same terms. By this time, Gary had $50 million in cash from the recent sale of a 304-acre, mixed-use property in Fort Worth, Texas. He had paid $35 million for the land as a 1031 exchange after the Archon sale.

Gary wired the money to Wolfswinkel and considered the loans as no-lose propositions. In his estimation, the properties Wolfswinkel acquired were prime investments that would bring healthy returns, and the interest rate was very attractive.

The major theme in this torrent of acquisitions and investments in 2006 was that they were well outside the hospitality industry, which Gary knew so well. Another such investment was Tharaldson Ethanol. As mentioned above, Kyle Newman was working for Gary and by 2006, he was assisting in land acquisition. Gary knew his family well. Kyle's grandfather Harold Newman founded Newman Signs, headquartered in Jamestown, which became highly successful and best known for its billboards. In the 1970s, Newman gained attention in the national media when he used his billboards for political comment. In response to President Jimmy Carter banning farmers from selling wheat to China and Russia, Newman commissioned billboards reading: "North Dakota Farmers Can't Live on Peanuts."

Tharaldson Ethanol near Casselton, ND, the fourth largest ethanol plant in the U.S.

Harold's son Russ took over the business, and Gary knew both men. Kyle Newman and Gary's son Matthew were close friends and had married sisters. The young men suggested that Gary build and run an ethanol plant, which they believed would be a solid investment because Harold had owned an ethanol plant in the 1980s in Grafton, North Dakota, north of Grand Forks near the Canadian border. It was one of the first ethanol plants in the U.S. and operated successfully for 28 years.

Congress created the renewable fuel standard (RFS) program as part of the Energy Policy Act of 2005 in order to reduce greenhouse gas emissions and grow the renewable fuels sector, while also reducing reliance on imported petroleum. RFS mandated that gasoline be blended with ethanol (currently, 10 percent), which is the cleanest burning and least expensive additive.

The timing for a new ethanol plant seemed perfect. In 2006, the margin on a gallon of ethanol was $1, which made operating a plant very profitable. Gary decided that Casselton, North Dakota, 25 miles west of Fargo, was the best location because of the plentiful supply of corn in the area, and the availability of natural gas and water needed to produce ethanol. The site is right on BNSF Railway's main line and only a mile from I-94. All the corn is produced locally (within 75 miles). Half of the corn is delivered by truck—up to 300 truckloads a day—and the other half is delivered by rail. Then the ethanol is transported in tankers from the plant to market.

Construction for the ethanol plant began in May 2007, and the plant went into production in January 2008. The Tharaldson Ethanol plant cost about $210 million to build, again from profits from sources other than the Archon sale. For example, in early 2007, Gary sold 14 acres of a 50-acre site on the Las Vegas Strip, about five miles south of McCarran International Airport, for $35 million, which was exactly what he paid for the entire 50 acres 15 months earlier.

The ethanol plant created 50 full-time jobs averaging over $50,000 per year, which were welcomed enthusiastically by the City of Casselton and its 2,300 residents. Farmers in the area were also very pleased to see the plant open.

Another large project with Gary's involvement came out of a 2003 partnership with DRG Properties in Las Vegas. Gary made an $80 million construction loan to DRG to build the Manhattan Luxury Condominiums (known as Manhattan I). The development consisted of 44 residential buildings with 700 total units and is located on the South Strip, about seven miles south of the intersection of Flamingo Road and Las Vegas Boulevard. The style is art deco, and the apartments sold for moderate prices ($200,000 to $400,000) for the area. Manhattan I opened in 2005 and Gary cleared $15 million, which was an 18 percent return in two years.

One of DRG's two main principals was Alex Edelstein, who made his fortune in high-tech, including participation in the design team for Microsoft Exchange and Microsoft Outlook. After the success of Manhattan I, Edelstein went out on his own as a real estate developer and initiated Manhattan West, which was a $350 million mixed-use project with 700 luxury condos and 200,000 square feet of restaurant, retail shopping, office and parking space. The 20-acre site is located in southwest Las Vegas.

Scott Financial put together a consortium of 29 banks in the fall of 2007 to participate in a construction loan of $110 million for the project. This time, Gary did not lend the money but agreed to guarantee the loan for a fee and interest on the loan amount. The construction of Manhattan West began in late 2007.

————————

From the close of the Archon deal, at the end of March 2006, until the first few months of 2007, Gary was consumed with deal-making, as described above, at the same time as he was recovering from two major surgeries. He worked diligently to wean himself off painkillers, taking half a pill when he could. But looking back at the period a decade later, Gary saw how acutely his judgment was affected by the healing process and the drugs. In a significant sense, making deals, which he loves to do, became a crutch that distracted him from physical and emotional pain as much as hydrocodone.

However, the effects of this crutch were not on Gary's mind as 2006 ended. Instead it was a time to celebrate a seemingly magical year. On December 19, 2006, Gary, Connie and three of their children (Dani, Bobbi and Gary, Jr.) flew to Cape Town, South Africa, with de Haan and his wife, Monica, and Jim Thomson, his wife, Margaret, and their three children. Back in March, on the evening before the Archon deal closed, Gary and Connie had hosted a dinner at Estiatoria Milos, an upscale Greek seafood restaurant in Midtown Manhattan. The guests included de Haan and his wife, Monica, who was pregnant with their son, and Jim Thompson and Margaret.

Gary thanked everyone for their efforts and patience throughout the deal's many challenges. During the meal, he said to de Haan, "Tell us more about South Africa."

De Haan described growing up in Cape Town and his parents and other family members who still lived there.

Gary was fascinated by de Haan's portrayal of his homeland, which could hardly be more different than Dazey—or anywhere in North Dakota. With the entire continent of Africa to the north, Cape Town is a port city on a peninsula with mountains to the west and the South Atlantic Ocean to the east and the Antarctic Ocean to the south. Inland, Gary imagined seeing lions, leopards, elephants, hippopotamuses, rhinoceroses and wildebeests—whatever those are.

"If the sale is successful tomorrow, let's go to South Africa," Gary suddenly said.

"That sounds great," de Haan replied. "You bring the plane, and I will bring the people." De Haan knew that Gary was in the process of buying his one rich man's luxury: a Gulfstream G450 jet, which had gone into production only two years earlier.

As if Gary needed another good thing to happen in 2006, Gulfstream gave him the larger G550 and a flight crew at no cost for the trip to South Africa. One might speculate that the company was enticing Gary to buy the more expensive G550 after the journey than the G450 he was in the process of purchasing.

The jet stopped only once to refuel in Puerto Rico. From there to Cape Town was the longest flight a G550 had ever taken, de Haan recalled. The entire flight from Las Vegas to Cape Town was 9,800 miles.

De Haan's parents and his grandfather, who had turned 100 years of age, greeted them at the airport. The group spent a week in Cape Town enjoying the hospitality of de Haan's family. Then they flew to Johannesburg to sightsee and visit two nature reserves for a week. From Johannesburg, they flew back to Las Vegas.

De Haan did not accompany the party to Johannesburg because his grandfather had taken a fall and he was visiting him in the hospital.

"We had a lovely time," said de Haan. "It was particularly moving for me because my grandfather died the day they flew back home."

De Haan was glad Gary had the opportunity to meet his grandfather. Both men and de Haan's father are people he admires greatly.

In 2007, Gary made another promising acquisition, the Las Vegas National Golf Club. The course gained renown when Tiger Woods won his first PGA golf tournament there on October 6, 1996. Gary invested $5 million, and another group put up $5 million as a down payment, and the partnership assumed a loan for $28 million to take ownership. The plan was to turn the golf course into an upscale housing development comprised of 532 lots.

Then Donald Trump contacted Gary about partnering to the course into a Trump golf course without a housing development. However, this partnership never came to fruition.

Now Gary had almost $1.3 billion invested in various ways in land and other projects outside the hotel business. He was also the guarantor of a construction loan for $110 million. Gary expected to make a return of 10 percent per year or more on these ventures, which would double his total investment within seven to eight years.

The sun was shining in Las Vegas, and there wasn't a cloud in sight on Gary's horizons in the dozen states where he owned land and hotels and was involved in other business.

But as happened in the New Testament, in the evening after the miracle of the loaves and fishes—when there was abundance—the disciples rowed out across the calm waters of the Sea of Galilee. In the deepest trough of night, a storm would arise without warning that was so furious these experienced fishermen were "tossed about while rowing, for the wind was against them." They would fear being thrown from the boat and then drowning.

CHAPTER THIRTEEN

Wandering in the Desert

Look alive. Here comes a buzzard.

Miz Beaver, Pogo

If you've never eaten while crying, you
don't know what life tastes like.

Johann Wolfgang von Goethe

MANHATTAN WEST was an ambitious project in southwest Las Vegas, as mentioned in the previous chapter. The goal was to construct 12 buildings with 700 luxury condos along with 150,000 square feet of office space and 50,000 square feet of retail space. The average condo price was projected to be $400,000.

Construction began in early 2008, unfortunately just as the Great Recession was taking hold. During the early 2000s, a nationwide housing boom precipitated a housing bubble, meaning that housing prices increased dramatically by almost two-thirds from 2000 to the beginning of 2007. Such a rapid increase in costs is often described as a bubble because eventually prices expand far beyond what the market can bear—and the bubble bursts.

Several states, including Arizona and Nevada, enjoyed especially hot markets with housing prices rising more than 80 percent. To a significant extent, the bubble was pumped up by high-risk financial practices, most notably sub-prime mortgages. Sub-prime mortgages are mortgages that lending institutions use for borrowers with low credit ratings. Since the risk of default is greater, banks and other lending brokers charge higher than conventional interest. These proved highly profitable for lenders, many of which indulged in issuing large numbers of "Ninja" loans—that is, loans to people without jobs, income or assets, and often with no money down.

Lax regulations and willful institutional blindness to the inevitable catastrophe allowed short-term profit-making to rule. But as soon as housing prices started declining, sub-prime mortgages, especially the Ninja variety were in deep trouble. Families without resources were soon saddled with houses that were worth much less than their mortgages. They couldn't sell their properties and break even, let alone make money as had been true as the housing bubble swelled. Pop! Boom!!

A recession began in late 2007 that within months impacted employment, closing all avenues of escape for people whose properties were under water. Foreclosures spread like a contagion, devastating communities. The Great Recession turned out to be the worst global recession since the Great Depression in the 1930s. In the U.S., 7.5 million jobs were lost as the unemployment rate doubled. The stock market plummeted wiping out $16 trillion of wealth in households nationwide.

Abandoned structures at the former Manhattan West project in southwest Las Vegas. Construction was suspended in December 2008. Photograph by Terrisa Meeks.

One of the hardest-hit areas was Las Vegas. Housing prices tumbled relentlessly at the same time as Manhattan West suffered construction problems (contractor liens from other projects and building code violations) that slowed completion of the project. By December 2008, the real estate market had completely collapsed in Las Vegas and construction was halted.

The disintegration of this project left Gary on a very expensive hook. He had guaranteed a construction loan for $110 million.

More troubles began closing in. Only two weeks earlier a second law suit was initiated against Gary regarding the ESOP. On November 13, 2008, Bernard McKay, et al. v. Tharaldson was filed as a class action suit alleging a breach of fiduciary duty under ERISA (Employee Retirement Income Security Act of 1974), a federal law regulating privately established health care and pension plans. This suit was a minor annoyance compared to the Hans law suit, filed in 2005, which was still active and proceeding towards a settlement or a trial, either of which might cost Gary $100 million or more.

In January 2009, Gary's lawyers filed a law suit against Scott Financial and the Bank of Oklahoma alleging, according to the Bismarck Tribune, "that the two groups withheld or misrepresented information about the project that violated conditions under which he and his companies would guarantee the loans. Among other issues, his suit alleges that minimum levels of occupancy and income from the project were not met as a condition of the guarantee. Also, the suit allege[d] that Scott took advantage of his close relationship with Tharaldson and his representation of him in previous deals to induce Tharaldson into participating in the $110 million financing package."

In August, the Bank of Oklahoma, a prime investor in the Manhattan West project, sued Gary to recoup its loan plus interest. The suit also alleged that Gary was liable for the entire $110 million. In November, a federal judge ruled that this suit against Gary could proceed.

In the spring of 2009, as Gary was dealing with the Manhattan West debacle, he called de Haan. "I have a problem with the ethanol plant," he said.

"What's the problem?" de Haan asked.

Gary explained that he had a loan for $58 million on the plant with Bank of America, which was demanding a collateral enhancement and an unreasonable paydown. The original letter of credit involved tax-exempt bonds and was established with LaSalle Bank, which had been taken over by the Bank of America. The collateral issue was understandable since the funds had been secured using Gary's CityView property, the value of which had plummeted from $145 million in 2006 to $19 million because of the recession. But the timeframe for paydown was too demanding, especially in light of the difficulties at the ethanol plant.

Tharaldson Ethanol had opened on time at the beginning of 2008. But it could only run at 40 to 50 percent efficiency because the drying system for the distiller's grain, which is produced from mashing the corn to produce ethanol, functioned poorly. Distiller's grain from corn is a high-protein livestock feed and accounts for 20 percent of the plant's revenue.

"We tried a new drying technology that was successful in the sugar beet industry," said Ryan Thorpe, CEO of Tharaldson Ethanol. "If they had proven efficient, the dryers would have greatly improved productivity."

However, the dryers proved ineffective with corn since it contains significantly more moisture than beets. Repairs on the dryers were expensive and time-consuming.

At the same time, the perfect financial storm hit. Corn prices shot up to $8 per bushel. In comparison, the same bushel sold for $3.50 in September 2017. This had a dramatic impact on profitability for a plant like Tharaldson's that grinds 50 million bushels per year.

As well, there was an oversupply of ethanol as other plants came on line. Then the Great Recession took hold and ethanol prices fell. The profit on ethanol sank from $1 per gallon, which was quite profitable when construction began, to $0.1 per gallon. Gary had expected to generate enough return from the ethanol plant to cover the soft and hard costs involved in preparing his land holdings for sale. If the plant was operating at full capacity producing 13 million gallons of ethanol a month, Gary thought he would be clearing more than $8.33 million a month (or $100 million per year) at 2006 ethanol prices, which would have solved much of his liquidity challenges. Gary knew that ethanol prices would rise again after the ongoing recession; people would be able to drive more miles, which would force up the price of gasoline. But that seemed centuries away at present.

De Haan contacted the Bank of America and was able to negotiate better terms. Additional land had to be put up as collateral, and the bank demanded the bond be paid down as these properties were sold. There provided more breathing room for Gary but blocked access to cash from the sale of the collateral holdings.

At mid-2009, the plant was still running at half-capacity. The dryers were under warranty, but the manufacturing company had gone out of business. Gary asked his engineering and maintenance staff at the plant if they believed the dyers could ever be fixed. They answered no. Gary decided that the best and only realistic option was to have conventional dryers installed—for $40 million, after losing $20 million due to the plant's poor performance.

The problem was that Gary didn't have the cash to refit the plant, and credit was going to be difficult to acquire, especially on favorable terms, from banks. De Haan and his partner Jim Thompson at CFC looked elsewhere and were able to secure a loan from Doherty Funding LLC, a commercial lending firm.

Tharaldson Ethanol running at full capacity on a winter's night. The plant produces 165 million gallons of ethanol per year.

By February 2010, new conventional dryers were installed and the ethanol plant was running at full capacity for the first time. The profit was modest that year and not the cash cow he had hoped for. But at least the plant was distilling corn into alcohol instead of time and bushels of money into frustration.

Also around February 2010—and just after the Manhattan West project had been shut down, which was weighing heavily on Gary's mind—he called Warren again.

"I have all these assets but no liquidity," Gary said. "I need cash."

Gary had salaries to pay and huge legal costs in the ESOP and Manhattan West lawsuits. Also, major expenditures were required to get his landholdings in shape to sell. The market would rebound eventually and Gary had to be ready to take advantage. Much of the land he bought for residential, commercial and retail development needed to be entitled, which would cost about $50 million in total. Other "soft costs" included creating master plans for a resort or housing development, for example. There were also about $25 million in "hard costs" to absorb for roads, trails, community centers and sales facilities at resort and other properties. At the same time, Gary was paying $2 million to $3 million a year in taxes on the landholdings.

"Why don't you sell some hotels?" de Haan replied.

De Haan reviewed Gary's balance sheet and determined there were several hotels he could sell. Over the next two years, de Haan arranged for the sale of four hotels (two Residence Inns, one Homewood Suites and one Courtyard Inn) to Apple REIT, a publicly traded real estate investment trust. Apple REIT currently has one of the largest hotel portfolios in the U.S. with 237 hotels, which is 58 percent of the number of hotels Gary built by the end of 2008. In total, the hotels sold for $65 million, which was very helpful and also illustrated Gary's predicament.

All four hotels were relatively new and doing well financially despite the recession, precisely because Gary and his staff had chosen good sites and then ran the hotels efficiently while maintaining the top customer satisfaction ratings in the industry. The hotels were designed to withstand economic downturns. This was obvious to buyers who were willing to pay $16.25 million on average for each property. The hotels would have sold for 20 percent more in 2006, but their decline in value due to the recession wasn't as severe as the plummet in the value of Gary's landholdings.

As the Great Recession cascaded through the real estate industry, Gary opened seven hotels in 2008 and three more hotels in 2009. Construction on these had already begun, and they were designed to withstand economic downturns.

Gary also owned 29 sites in 13 states from New York to California, where he was planning to build hotels in the next few years. But it would be impossible now to get construction loans for new projects, and Gary was running out of capital to invest as equity.

Instead of hosting new hotels serving thousands of customers, providing hundreds of new jobs and generating $100 million in revenue for every 20 to 25 hotels, these sites were now empty lots literally collecting dust.

In the spring of 2010, as de Haan was working on selling Gary's four hotels, Gary called again.

"I've got another problem I need you to fix," he said.

"Okay, what is it?" de Haan answered.

"I made this $70 million loan three years ago to a guy in Arizona," Gary replied. "His name is Conley Wolfswinkel." Gary explained that Wolfswinkel made a year of interest payments and then stopped. All of his assets were land that, as Gary was experiencing, had no liquidity in a deep recession. Gary's loan was on property that was now worth much less than the loan. Worse, the unpaid interest would soon amount to $30 million.

"Warren, I need you to go and look at this thing and tell me what you think," Gary said.

De Haan agreed and began researching Wolfswinkel.

"After due diligence investors wouldn't typically lend him that kind of money," de Haan said. "And to think Gary lent Wolfswinkel $70 million after knowing him for only about seven days. Gary is a very trusting guy. If someone calls and says they have a great deal, he will listen. It's actually a shortcoming because it's made him vulnerable to people who didn't have the credibility to sell what they were peddling."

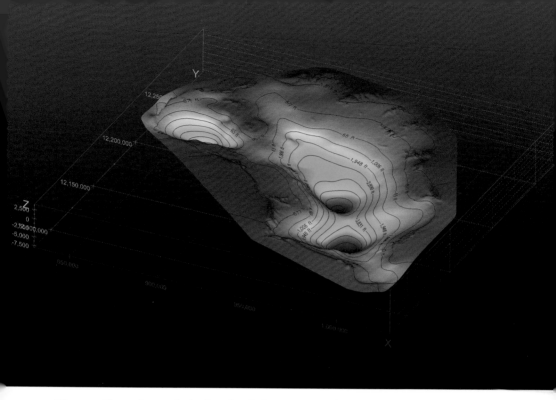

The acquifer underneath the farmland Gary owns in the Harquahala Valley 70 miles from Phoenix, AZ. The acquifer is deeper than the Grand Canyon at its deepest point.

Fortunately, Wolfswinkel wasn't one such character. The danger was that he would declare bankruptcy and Gary would lose most or maybe all of his investment. When de Haan met Wolfswinkel, he was impressed by the man and the "terrific lieutenants who worked for him. They were very smart and honest guys."

De Haan was pleasantly surprised to discover that "Wolfswinkel had come up with a decent plan, not for bankruptcy, but a long-term strategy."

What Gary didn't know when he made the loan was that underneath the land in the Harquahala Valley is a large aquifer with twice as much water as currently in Lake Mead (on the Nevada-Arizona border) or Lake Powell (on the Utah-Arizona border), the largest two man-made aquifers in the U.S. The aquifer holds enough water to serve 350,000-500,000 households for a century. The estimated value of this resource is currently more than $1 billion.

The Harquahala Valley sits only 70 miles from Phoenix, which like Tucson, Arizona, is located in a desert. Rapid urbanization in and around these two

The Central Arizona Project canal (illustrated as a bold blue line running southeast over southern Arizona) runs directly through the Harquahala Valley.

cities, where most people in the state live, has outpaced available surface water supplies and the ongoing depletion of aquifers.

The groundwater in Harquahala is only 1,000 feet below surface level, which eases access. Also, the Central Arizona Project (CAP) canal, which transports water from the Colorado River to Central Arizona, runs right through the Harquahala Valley. This provides the infrastructure to deliver the water to Phoenix and Tucson. A small canal would have to be built to connect the aquifer to CAP, but the cost would be only $50 million—as opposed to the billions of dollars that would be needed if there was no CAP.

Neither Gary nor Wolfswinkel had $50 million on hand to build a canal, which was moot at that point. First, what is termed wheeling rights would have to be secured before water could be drawn from the aquifer and sold. However, it was obvious to both men that the aquifer added tremendous value to the property.

Wolfswinkel also proposed developing solar fields on sections of the land

Gary and Connie's house in Las Vegas, NV. The 15,800-square-foot home has 10 bedrooms, 12 bathrooms, two spiral staircases and a four-car garage with a motor court.

since it is the perfect combination of sunny, hot and flat.

Negotiations began with de Haan's visit, which both Gary and Wolfswinkel wanted to end well. Both wanted to retain as much value as they could for the long term. Bankruptcy would endanger that outcome for both.

After several rounds of negotiations over two years, which ended with Gary and Wolfswinkel meeting in New York, they agreed to terms: Gary reduced the amount owed from $100 to $60 million and took possession of the property. Also, Wolfswinkel agreed to give him 80 percent of revenue from the aquifer after the outstanding $60 million was paid off in full. The debt-for-equity swap relieved pressure on Wolfswinkel since he had only to pay off the principal and Gary agreed not to charge any more interest. And there was some hope for the future. The Great Recession wiped out Wolfswinkel's original $96 million investment in the property, but if wheeling rights are secured then he can make some of his money back and perhaps all of it in the long run.

"Basically we said we need control of this deal," de Haan recalled. "We needed to avoid any situation where Wolfswinkel would file bankruptcy."

However, the arrangement did little to help solve the immediate cash drought both entrepreneurs faced. Harquahala Valley was no longer an investment albatross, but as Samuel Taylor Coleridge penned, "Water, water everywhere, but not a drop to drink."

Most of the properties Gary invested in are located in desert areas in Nevada, Arizona and California. If not for water irrigating what is now farmland in Arizona, most of the state would still be desert or semi-desert. If not for water brought from long distances, cities such as Las Vegas and Phoenix would still be just dusty, desert crossroads.

Now Gary owned large quantities of land he couldn't develop and water he couldn't access. His hopes were wandering in an arid, inhospitable economic landscape, and his endurance was wilting under reality's unrelenting heat.

During this period, Gary's cash crunch became so severe that he and Connie put their home on the west side of Las Vegas up for sale. Again, the problem was that real estate prices had crashed. They couldn't find anyone interested in purchasing their $12 million home, even for half that amount. Gary sold his beloved Gulfstream G450 for $28 million two years after buying it for $34 million. Connie was contemplating going back to work as a schoolteacher to generate money to live on.

"Part of my frustration at this time was how difficult it was for Gary to adjust to market realities," de Haan said. "He told me to go sell the Harquahala Valley property for $1 billion." De Haan researched the actual value of the acreage at the time and then had to tell Gary it was only worth $60 million. And he doubted he could find anyone to buy it for that price.

Gary had become so accustomed to his holdings increasing by 10 percent per year, he struggled to come to terms with this new reality that was getting worse every day.

The lowest point was not only that Gary's lawyer was telling him he had to declare bankruptcy, but he had become convinced he couldn't escape that fate. In fact, on his lawyer's advice, he resigned as CEO of his own companies by the end of 2010 and put Kyle Newman in charge to avoid negative complications if Chapter 11 proceedings became unavoidable.

CHAPTER FOURTEEN

Return of the Hedgehog

Wisdom is knowing what to do next,
virtue is doing it

Robertson Davies

One of the very best of all earthly
possessions is self-possession.

George D. Prentice

AFTER THE SALE of most of the 140 hotels to Archon, Gary transformed from being a highly successful hedgehog to becoming a fox dabbling in businesses he knew little about. Then, as a major economic downturn deepened, he became the red fox in the foxhunt. Chasing after him were creditors, lawyers and schemers. With over $1 billion invested in non-liquid assets, the wily fox seemed more like a sitting duck. How could Gary become a hedgehog again?

There is a Japanese Zen play in which a pregnant woman crawls to the middle of the stage. A baby's voice pleads, "Let me out. Let me out." The mother responds, "Let yourself out."

———————————

On a Friday in mid-2009, de Haan answered his cell phone and Gary was on the line.

"I want you to come to the ESOP mediation with me in Napa on Sunday," Gary said. "Also, there are some documents you will need to read."

"Well, this sounds interesting," de Haan replied. "Sure, I'll go with you and see what's up."

Soon after de Haan hung up, he received hundreds of pages of text regarding the Hans lawsuit to read. When de Haan met Gary at a resort hotel in Napa, California, he could see right away that "this was the darkest of times when the ESOP litigation was torturing Gary. He was spending a fortune on legal fees, and the lawyers were unreasonable."

Gary and de Haan went to the mediation meeting, which was a room swarming with lawyers—or were they sharks? It was not only hard to tell, but worse, de Haan soon realized that none of the "killer" lawyers were on their side. Representing the plaintiffs were top litigators. "These were some of the best and highest-paid litigators in the world, sharpshooters," de Haan recalled. The same was true for the legal team representing the interests of TMI, which was not seeking to harm Gary but to protect the company's liability in the lawsuit. In that mission, they were not there to help Gary either.

Gary was clearly frustrated after dealing for several years with implacable law teams who showed no understanding of the fundamental fact that the

ESOP was a gift to his employees. De Haan saw the effect of the mounting pressures on Gary. "He was visibly exhausted and in severe pain," de Haan observed.

"Tally-ho" seemed to be the unspoken yet resounding cry bouncing off the walls of the room and throughout Gary's affairs. The phrase originated in the Middle Ages as a French battle cry: taille (the cutting edge of a sword) and haut (raised up) meaning "swords up." This idiom eventually became anglicized as "tally-ho" and used in hunting, especially in the foxhunt. In World War II, tally-ho was used to pilots to communicate that an enemy fighter plane had been sighted.

In England, red foxes were used for the hunt because they were much easier for mounted riders to see. Gary's troubles were painting him crimson.

The plaintiffs' lawyers in the Hans case had originally sought more than $200 million. Four years of litigation later and Gary's lawyers had succeeded in lowering the demand by only $50 million. Gary considered any amount to be rapacious and de Haan agreed. Worse, Gary didn't have $150 million to pay out after a settlement. He was also still in litigation regarding the Manhattan West construction loan, with $110 million in liability, and his land assets were still far from recovering their value.

The mediation meeting began and "the judge was trying to force a settlement, which is what they do," de Haan recalled. "Gary was clearly distraught. I went into a few settlement meetings separately where the other side's lawyers were very skilled and very firm."

Back in mediation, de Haan saw that "the difference between our litigators and theirs was like the difference between the city all-star basketball team and a C-level high school team."

Gary's lawyers suggested he should settle and get it over with.

"Are you mad?" de Haan exclaimed. "Where do you come from spending this guy's money? Don't you realize how distraught he is?"

De Haan turned to Gary and said, "I think I know what we need to do." They left the meeting and as they walked away, de Haan said, "We need to change lawyers."

What de Haan didn't say was that this scenario was where Gary's frugality was hurting him. But over lunch, Gary agreed with the need for new repre-

Gary and Connie with children and grandchildren at the family lake house in western Minnesota. Back row (left to right), Gary II, Grant, Connie. Front row (left to right), Louis, Matthew, Joey, Lucy, Izzy, Bobbi, Dani, Gary.

sentation and the reality that he was going to have to pay a lot more for a top-notch team.

Gary and de Haan went back to mediation, and Gary stood up to say, "There is nothing more for us to talk about now. We are leaving."

"Everyone there was dumbfounded," de Haan recalled. "Lawyers slamming their pens on the table and saying, 'I can't understand this.'"

This was a profound moment of clarity for Gary; the hunted needed to become the hunter. To do so, he had to find the strength to stand up for himself despite feeling chased and badgered to the point of exhaustion by platoons of legal and financial foxhounds. If his wife or one of his children were in trouble, he would spare no expense to provide the most capable legal defense and offense. Now, with de Haan's urging, he was restored to the hedgehog's certainty about who he was and what he stood for.

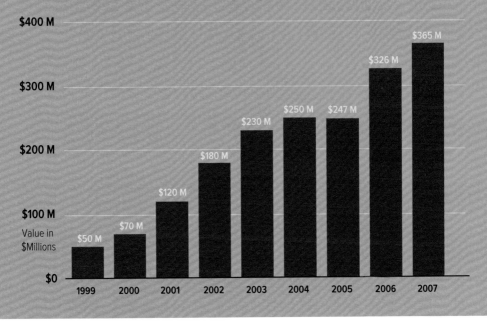

Increase in ESOP Equity Value 1999-2007

Value in $Millions

Year	Value
1999	$50 M
2000	$70 M
2001	$120 M
2002	$180 M
2003	$230 M
2004	$250 M
2005	$247 M
2006	$326 M
2007	$365 M

De Haan called Jim Thompson and said, "Jimmy, we need to get on this thing immediately." Thompson recommended Proskauer Rose LLP, which was founded in New York City in 1875. Proskauer Rose has often been recognized as one of the top legal firms in the country, most recently in The American Lawyer and U.S. News & World Report.

After an interview process, Gary was represented by Howard Shapiro and Robert Rachal at Proskauer Rose. "It was the best move we ever made," said de Haan.

Shapiro and Rachal reviewed the lawsuits and, by the end of 2011, laid out clearly that Gary was in a very strong position to win at trial—which was exceptional in such cases. In fact, there were no grounds for Gary to settle for a penny. The evidence was indisputable that TMI did not overpay for the ESOP. On June 17, 2002, Thomas A. Furlong, the president of APEX Financial Services, Inc., submitted an evaluation of the ESOP to TMI. He noted that "the ESOP paid $50 million in cash and issued $447.46 million in promissory notes to [Gary]. ... Outstanding ESOP-related debt totaled $473.51 million on December 31, 2001." Furlong's evaluation agreed with the original valuation at the time of sale. To top it off, the plaintiffs' expert had only one minor disagreement with Furlong's work.

In the table above, another evaluation in 2008 showed that the ESOP gained $365 million in equity in eight years. After paying debt service and other expenses, revenue from the hotels Gary sold to the ESOP added $45.6 million per year on average to the equity that belonged to ESOP members.

This dramatic increase in equity was due, as noted in Chapter 10, to the excellent fiscal performance of the hotels, as measured by RevPar, EBITDA and comparisons with competitors. This performance was exactly why Whitehall was negotiating to buy all the ESOP hotels in 2006 for $1.215 billion at the same time as Archon was doing the same regarding Gary's hotels. The sale didn't materialize because of the Hans lawsuit. Then when real estate markets collapsed nationwide, the deal was completely abandoned.

In 2011 and 2012, as Shapiro and Rachal were wearing down the plaintiffs' litigation team, Gary's wife Connie was helping him regain his footing vis-à-vis bankruptcy. Although Gary's lawyers were advising strongly to declare, she was adamant that this route did not accord with who he is. It was clearly her husband's nature to stand and fight, rather than flee. Even if he could run as fast as a fox, even if he was cunning and deceptive, the dogs would likely win anyway. They pursue relentlessly until the fox is so exhausted and dispirited, he gives in—just as Gary was almost ready to do at the ESOP mediation in Napa.

"I didn't marry you for your money," Connie said. "It's alright if we lose it all. But we don't want bankruptcy on our record. It's about doing what's right."

Gary agreed and later said, "Connie has way more common sense than I do." He consulted with her lawyers on Garman Turner Gordon LLP in Las Vegas.

"You want to pay back the banks anyway," Greg Garman said after listening to Gary. "So let's work it out. The banks believed in you all these years. Go, sit down and have a talk with them about how to repay the loans."

Gary met with his bankers to work out repayment. His net worth had fallen almost by half from $1.66 billion in 2006 to $868 million at the end of 2011. This improved by 2 percent by the end of 2012, which was hopeful at least The recession was over but recovery was in no rush.

Gary had built his success on quick decisions and fast results. Patience was not a strength. Fortunately, when anyone needs patience, it's always there waiting.

Gary also called on friends to help him hang on until he could sell properties and restore liquidity. Bruce White, his longtime friend and fellow hotel developer, lent Gary $10 million.

"That was the easiest decision ever," White said. "If you understood how much I owe to Gary for White Lodging and my own personal success, you would understand that was a very easy thing to do."

Another friend, a banker Gary had done business with and knew personally, lent him $5 million to help him endure.

"In 2009, we couldn't get an offer for any property," Gary recalled. "In 2010, all we got was lowball offers. Then in 2011, we got contracts to buy on the land, but nobody would close. And we were spending a lot of money on lawyers trying to do the contracts. In 2012, we started to get close to the amount of money on offers that we paid for properties."

Twenty-five hundred years ago, Greek playwright Euripides wrote, "Second thoughts are ever wiser." In 2010 and 2011, when Gary had relinquished control of his companies to Kyle Newman, he had plenty of time for the age-old practice of second thoughts. Humanity's challenge today, as in antiquity, is to have first thoughts.

"When I sold my company to Archon in 2006, I made a really big mistake," Gary observed, "because then I focused on doing other things that I believed I could do extremely well. But I never had the passion. Of course, the economy played a role. Meanwhile, the hotel business performed well during the downturn."

Gary likened himself to "a kid with too much cash. I blew it on companies I really didn't know how to run well. I hired people I thought could do the job but was often disappointed."

As well, three factors converged to dampen the sense of caution that should have awakened as Gary ventured into unfamiliar business territory.

Gary sharing lunch and a laugh on the deck of the family lake house with Dani (left) and other children and grandchildren.

First, he had overcome the fear of failure so thoroughly after it stymied his first attempt to sell insurance in the 1970s that it never occurred to Gary that he could fail at anything. In a verbal nutshell, that encapsulated Gary's hubris.

"As a real estate guy, I believe in property as an investment," said Blagg. "It's a lot harder to get hurt when you have a deed. If you buy stock or make almost any other kind of investment, you run the risk of that asset going to zero. Land might not have liquidity in a down market, but someday it's going to be worth something."

Gary understood this and, in fact, hotels are a type of real estate. But they retain liquidity. "I overdid it with raw land," Gary remarked. "A few hundred million dollars would have been alright."

The second factor quelling Gary's natural restraint was the painkillers he was taking as he bought so much land.

Thirdly, he was operating outside his normal checks and balances. Fyke, Larson and others were not working with him after the Archon sale. Blagg had just started working for Gary and like Don Cape, who also oversaw Gary's finances, he was in the position of reacting to Gary's decisions rather than participating in his decision-making.

As Blagg perceived, Gary's capacity to tolerate risk was a crucial component of his success. As Gary put it often, "I didn't feel I was ever doing anything risky because I knew what I was doing."

In addition, he had built risk insurance into the operational efficiency of his hotels. "Our hotel business can take a pretty good hit and still make debt-service coverage and generate enough money to operate," Blagg said. "If RevPar goes down by 10 or 15 percent, we're not happy about it, but we're still fine because our debt levels are conservative."

Blagg pointed out the importance of understanding leverage. "You can't build any business and get rich without using leverage, but you have to keep borrowing within smart parameters."

"Bill Marriott had this thing about sticking to your knitting, sticking to your core business," Gary said. He recounted how Marriott learned the hard way—just as he was doing—how important sticking to one's knitting is. Marriott Corporation got into financial trouble when it ventured into other industries, such as the amusement park business.

After another year and a half of negotiations during which Shapiro and Rachal were wearing down the plaintiffs' legal team, a settlement was reached. Gary was intent on going to trial for total victory, but it was more important to get the ESOP lawsuits out of the way. By 2013, the economy was well on the way to recovery and real estate markets were gaining momentum. Now was the time to put the ESOP hotels up for sale again so members could cash out. Many workers were at retirement age or approaching the end of their careers.

The Hans case was terminated on February 25, 2013. Gary agreed to settle—not for $200 million or $100 million or $50 million, but for $15 million. This turned out to be close to a wash for Gary. He was awarded $9 million in a suit he initiated against the firm that had originally—and mistakenly—set up the ESOP beginning in 1998. The first $10 million in Gary's legal fees had been covered by TMI's indemnification insurance, which applied to Gary as CEO. He spent considerably more when he engaged Proskauer and Rose, but that was money very well spent.

However, Gary was paid several million dollars in interest on an $11

Connie pilots the family pontoon boat in front of the lake house with Gary II, Gary, Dani, Lucy and other family members.

million note he was carrying for TMI. Forgiving the principal on that note was part of the $15 million settlement.

The McKay law suit was also terminated on February 25, 2013. According to court documents, this suit alleged that Gary should have sued himself "for the 'misuse, dissipation and misappropriation' of approximately $4 million in TMI assets that were paid to his ex-wife. … Plaintiffs contend this dissipation and waste of TMI assets from 1998 until 2007 resulted in a diminution in the value of TMI stock." At issue was the 20-year consulting contract TMI gave to Gary's ex-wife, Linda, on March 28, 1998. The judge ruled that "the TMI ESOP did not own any shares of company stock" at that time because it was not established until the following year. The ruling also stated that Gary "was not a fiduciary when the consulting agreement was executed and, therefore, there is no viable cause of action under ERISA."

To prevent any further action, Gary agreed to settle the McKay suit for $125,000. Now the way was clear to sell the ESOP for the members' benefit.

"I did it for the employees," said Gary, "and I want to be alive to see how it benefits them."

CHAPTER FIFTEEN

Bases Loaded

Work and play are words used to
describe the same thing under
different circumstance.

Mark Twain

Underlying most arguments against
the free market is a lack of belief
in freedom itself.

Milton Friedman

ASKELADDEN IS THE UNLIKELY HERO in many Norwegian folktales who represents the small, everyday man who succeeds because of his wits where others fail. The name Askeladden literally means "Ash Lad" signifying his low stature. In traditional households that were heated by burning wood in a fireplace, the person least fit for other tasks was assigned the job of watching over the hearth and blowing in the ashes (or embers) to keep the fire from going out.

While Gary was not the least among his brothers and sisters (albeit the shortest brother), he was certainly at a disadvantage compared to many other youngsters in his generation in terms of material wealth and evident talent. He was a passionate but not gifted athlete, which prevented from pursuing his first love, professional baseball. Throughout high school and university, Gary was a B or C student. He graduated on time but without shining academically. Nor was he interested in typical creative pursuits, such as music or art.

But once in the real world, confronted with challenges, Gary's brilliance began to show. In Norwegian folktales, Askeladden's brothers fail to save the princess and other tasks because they are stuck in traditional thinking. But Askeladden thinks strategically and is far more observant of the reality of his situation. He devises tactics to outsmart trolls, fend off monsters and take control of a magical Viking ship to rescue the princess.

Similarly, Gary was not bound by conventional approaches to the lodging industry and, as shown in previous chapters, figured out creative ways to succeed—and he did it on his own, starting from zero. After the Archon sale in 2006, he put himself into a situation that was foreign to his knowledge base, and he struggled. Once Gary rediscovered his hedgehog persona, he transitioned from the exhaustion and despair of feeling chased by packs of howling hounds back to the strategic thinking that earned him success.

———

At the beginning of 2011, Gary asked Aimee Fyke to come back to work for him and manage the 23 hotels he still owned. Almost three years earlier, she had gone to work for Archon to manage hospitality assets and, after experiencing corporate bureaucracy, was thrilled to be able to go back to work for Gary. In February 2011, Fyke became the COO of Gary's new company,

"Askeladdens Adventure" by Theodor Kittelsen (1857-1914). The original painting is owned by the National Library of Norway.

Tharaldson Hospitality Management (THM), and set up THM's operations office in Decatur, Illinois, where she had lived since 1991.

This was the worst period of Gary's career. He was grasping at both hope and trust. "To me, this is very personal and speaks to Gary's loyalty to his people," Fyke said. In fact, Gary founded THM specifically to get her to return. TMI was still managing his hotels and doing so well. But Gary wanted better—the best—which he believed only Fyke could provide.

As soon as economic growth returned, Gary planned to build more hotels, to resume his knitting—if he could keep himself financially afloat long enough. For these were the Obama years when the Gross Domestic Product (GDP) grew at 1.5 percent per year, which was the slowest rate since 1933. In comparison, the GDP under President Ronald Reagan was 3.5 percent; 2.1 percent for President George Bush, Sr.; 3.9 percent for President Bill Clinton; and 2.3 percent for President George H.W. Bush. Unlike the aftermath of previous major economic downturns, economic recovery was tepid following the Great Recession. In addition, new federal regulations increased the burden of doing business by more than $100 billion from 2008 to 2015. This helped create an economic environment that inhibited growth, and all the land Gary bought for development required fiscal growth to attract buyers.

The ESOP settlement was reached in February 2013, and then Gary's liability for Manhattan West project was determined in May. Gary agreed to pay $85 million to lenders in a structured settlement. Although he felt he'd been taken advantage of, he did not want to alienate the banking sector that had been so crucial to his success in the past and would be just as important to building his third empire. Gary could have declared bankruptcy and walked away from the Manhattan West fiasco, as his lawyers were advising in 2011 and 2012 before he retained Garman. It is not unusual for developers and speculators to do so when a large project tanks. But doing the right thing vis-à-vis banks is a foundational principle for Gary. Despite very real pressures pushing him towards bankruptcy, he sought a more honorable solution.

The structured settlement did not involve any cash from Gary, which was in short supply. Instead the banks agreed to be repaid by proceeds from the sale of the ESOP, which owed Gary $300 million, and from Harquahala water rights.

"Manhattan West was a big mess," said Joe Blagg, "and at the end of the day everybody took a haircut. Obviously, Gary took the biggest haircut." To the credit of the banks, they agreed to terms that Gary could fulfill, including paying off the principal of $85 million plus a reasonable interest rate.

From 1982 through 2005, Gary built two hotel empires: the first (214 hotels) he sold to the ESOP in 1999, and the second (140 hotels) he sold to Archon in 2006. Together, both empires totaled 350 hotels that were worth about $2.5 billion. In total, Gary built 394 hotels during this period and bought 18 additional hotels. He also sold 62 hotels.

When Fyke rejoined Gary in 2011, he had 23 hotels consisting of 12 hotels not included in the Archon deal and 11 hotels built from 2007 to 2009. Although Gary was running out of cash, these lodgings were already underway and would generate income. He also mothballed 27 prospective hotel sites for future development. By the end of 2012, he had sold four hotels to Apple REIT, as noted in Chapter Thirteen.

The Fyke family in October 2016. From left, Sydney, Ryan, Aimee, Addison, Tim and Danielle.

In 2012, Gary knew that the ESOP lawsuits would be resolved with little or no cost beyond legal fees. He also reached an agreement in principle regarding the Manhattan West debacle, which was executed seven months later. As well that year, there was more interest from developers and land speculators in Gary's landholdings. Deals weren't closing yet, but it seemed they would in the near future.

As a result, Gary felt confident enough to break ground on two new hotels. Eighteen months later, on October 14, 2013, Gary opened a Residence Inn with 101 rooms in Largo, Maryland. Five days later, he opened a Residence Inn with 106 rooms in Albany, New York.

These were the first hotels Gary had built in more than four years. The question reverberating throughout the hospitality industry was, "Is Gary back?"

Gary opened three hotels in 2014, and he did the same the following year. From 1990 through 2009, Gary averaged 19 new hotels per year—peaking at 46 hotels in 1995. Now he was building at a pace that was six times slower than the 20-year average and 15 times slower than his top tempo.

From left, Joe Blagg, Development & Finance Manager and Don Cape,
Vice President of Western Development at Tharaldson Hospitality Management.

Maybe Gary should have retired rather than make a feeble comeback. Maybe Gary had lost his touch.

But Gary had a plan. As he lay awake at night during the Great Recession and its lethargic aftermath, he thought deeply about how to reenter the hotel business. This time, he was determined to build a significant portfolio again—but to keep, not to sell. This new lodging group would be built to survive and prosper for 40 or 50 years, and they would be central to Gary's business legacy. In total, Gary envisioned building 31 to 40 new hotels to get to 50 hotels in total by the end of 2020.

The new strategy involved building hotels in high-barrier locations—that is, in larger urban areas where land costs are high and available sites are few. It costs a lot more to build there, but Gary was also choosing sites where demand is high. The scarcity and high cost of land serve to keep competition out, not just at present but also in the foreseeable future. Instead of building in areas where multiple sites were available, Gary would choose areas that were already developed for the most part. No other developer would be able

THARALDSON HOSPITALITY HOTEL PROPERTIES–2017

● Hotels Under Development

CALIFORNIA
Homewood Suites–Bakersfield
Homewood2–Bakersfield
Staybridge Suites–Bakersfield
Residence Inn–Brea
Springhill Suites–Lake Forest
TownPlace Suites–Lake Forest
Homewood Suites–Livermore
Residence Inn–Livermore
Springhill Suites–Newark
Staybridge Suites–Newark
Residence Inn–Novato
Springhill Suites–Ontario
Homewood2–Ontario
Staybridge Suites–Ontario
Hilton Inn & Suites–Porter Ranch
Homewood Suites–Rancho Cordova
Residence Inn–Redlands
Residence Inn– Roseville
Homewood2–Roseville
Element Hotels–Sacramento
Staybridge Suites–San Bernardino
Hilton Inn & Suites–Santa Rosa
Residence Inn–Santa Rosa
Staybridge Suites–Temecula
Hilton Garden Inn–Walnut Creek

COLORADO
Hilton Garden Inn–Broomfield
Homewood Suites–Broomfield

IDAHO
Staybridge Suites–Coeur d'Alene

MARYLAND
Hilton Garden Inn–Arundel Mills
Homewood Suites–Arundel Mills
Residence Inn–Richie Station

MICHIGAN
Hyatt House–Grand Rapids
Residence Inn–Grand Rapids

NEVADA
Candlewood Suites–Las Vegas
Holiday Inn Express–Las Vegas
Homewood2–Las Vegas
TownPlace Suites–Las Vegas
Residence Inn–Sparks

NEW JERSEY
Residence Inn–Bridgewater
Springhill Suites–Bridgewater

NEW YORK
Hyatt House–Albany

NORTH CAROLINA
Staybridge Suites–Concord
Staybridge Suites–Raleigh

TENNESSEE
Hyatt House–Franklin
Staybridge Suites–Franklin
Hyatt House–Nashville
Staybridge Suites–Nashville

TEXAS
Hilton Garden Inn–Austin
TownPlace Suites–Austin
Homewood2–San Antonio

WASHINGTON
Springhill Suites–Spokane Airport

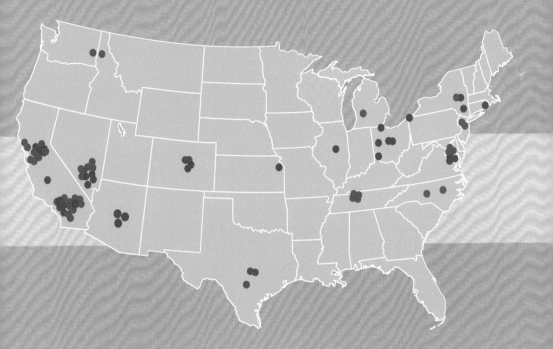

● Existing Hotels

ARIZONA
Staybridge Suites–Chandler
Hilton Garden Inn–Tempe
Homewood Suites–Tempe

ARKANSAS
Fairfield Inn–Little Rock
Residence Inn–Little Rock

CALIFORNIA
Residence Inn–Corona
Staybridge Suites–Corona
Fairfield Inn & Suites–Folsom
Staybridge Suites–Folsom
Courtyard–Rancho Cucamonga
Hilton Garden Inn–Rancho Cucamonga
Homewood Suites–Rancho Cucamonga
SpringHill Suites–Roseville
Towneplace Suites–Roseville
Staybridge Suites–Sacramento
Fairfield Inn & Suites–San Bernardino
Holiday Inn Express–Visalia

COLORADO
Residence Inn–Denver
Staybridge Suites–Denver

ILLINOIS
Residence Inn–Forsyth

KANSAS
Residence Inn–Kansas City

MARYLAND
Courtyard–Largo
Residence Inn–Largo

NEVADA
Hilton Garden Inn–Las Vegas
Holiday Inn Express–Las Vegas
Residence Inn–Las Vegas
Staybridge Suites–Las Vegas

NEW YORK
Courtyard–Kingston
Residence Inn–Albany

OHIO
Fairfield Inn & Suites–Cincinnati
Residence Inn–Columbus
Staybridge Suites–Columbus
Staybridge Suites–Maumee
Residence Inn–Dayton

PENNSYLVANIA
TownePlace Suites–Erie

RHODE ISLAND
Residence Inn–Greenwich

VIRGINIA
Residence Inn–Fredericksburg
Residence Inn–Springfield

to build nearby, which was especially tempting to competitors given Gary's reputation. With his new strategy, if there happened to be a site available next door, he would own it, too.

For example, the Residence Inn that opened in October 2013 is located in Largo, Maryland, a wealthy suburban area just outside the Capital Beltway circling Washington, D.C. Nearby is one of the University of Maryland's campuses, Largo Medical Center and a shopping mall. Next door to the Residence Inn there was room to build another hotel, which Gary did: a Courtyard Inn, which opened on December 27, 2015.

To get going, Gary took on partners for the first time on an equal owner-ship basis, since he had limited liquidity. As Askeladden did, he had to use what was available to reach his objective. As well, the cost of building a hotel is now about $20 million, four times the cost in 1990. For most of the hotels he built from 2013 into 2017, Gary ended up with 50 percent of the equity. Now he is assuming full ownership on most new hotels.

In order to ramp up production beyond three or four hotels per year, Gary needed to assemble the right pieces in the right places, like a chess master. Bringing Amy back was the first big step. Larry Madson came back to work as the Director of Hotel Construction, and Bruce Thune was available for telephone and other electronic installations. Many other tradesmen and contractors were eager to work with Gary again, especially if he geared up as did in the 1990s. Through tough economic travails, Joe Blagg and Don Cape, the Vice President of Western Development, stayed with Gary. Cape oversees Gary's development projects in Western states, and Madson oversees construction.

Increasing the construction pace also required much more capital than Gary had in 2013 and '14, especially since he wanted to operate as inde-pendently as possible. Fortunately, Starwood Capital Group was negotiating with TMI to buy the ESOP. Starwood is a global real estate investment firm, currently with more than $54 billion in assets under management, headquar-tered in Greenwich, Connecticut. The sale officially closed on January 30, 2015, for more than $1.2 billion.

The next day, Gary received $289 million, the balance of the money owed to him for the sale of his hotels to the ESOP.

"That day, we paid off all the bank debt of $125 million on the ethanol plant in five minutes," recounted Ryan Thorpe, the COO of Tharaldson Ethanol. He also recalled hearing champagne bottles pop and might have taken a sip.

After the new dryers were installed, the ethanol plant averaged $312.6 million in revenue from 2010 through 2016. Just this enterprise alone would make Gary one of the top entrepreneurs in North Dakota. The plant made money every year except 2012, when the EBITDA was -$11.3 million, due to high costs and low ethanol sale prices. Otherwise, Tharaldson Ethanol's EBITDA averaged $34 million per year during this period. The projected revenue and EBITDA are slightly lower than these averages at $300 million and $25 million, which reflect market conditions.

Once the debts on Tharaldson Ethanol were paid off, the plant obviously had no debt service and became a source of significant funding for Gary's new hotel empire. This completed a pleasantly ironic circle in that profits from his hotels provided the capital to build the plant and now the plant was helping Gary resume his first business love.

In 2013 and '14, Gary was finally able sell some of his landholdings. The pace of making land deals picked up in 2015 through 2017. Some land Gary sold at a loss, other pieces he was happy to break even and some deals generated considerable profits. In April 2017, for example, he sold the five resort holdings in Colorado and Texas for a $5 million loss. No doubt these properties will make the buyers money, but they require further investments and expertise in this area of real estate development that Gary doesn't possess or seek.

In April 2016, Gary sold an 85-acre undeveloped mixed-use site in a suburban area north of Fort Worth, Texas, for $15.7 million. He bought the land for $14.3 million in 2006 and making a 10 percent profit is exactly what he planned to make on a per year basis—not over 10 years. However, Gary was able to negotiate to keep three acres for a future hotel site.

Gary paid $25.9 million for a 314-acre property zoned for single-family residences in Douglas County, Colorado. He invested an additional $12.4

million mostly in entitlement costs and then sold the property in tranches from 2013 through 2016 for $51.6 million.

In total, revenue for land sales totaled $160 million from 2013 through September 2017. Gary invested most of this money, along with proceeds from the ethanol plant and $164 million from the ESOP sale into hotel development.

Gary continues to sell his landholdings. Negotiations are currently underway to sell a mixed-use property for a profit of $40 million. Going forward, Gary no longer needs to sell his properties, but he would prefer to unload them so he can devote himself and his company to building and operating hotels.

He hasn't decided whether to keep the Harquahala Valley farmland. The aquifer underneath could benefit his family greatly for generations. On the other hand, an attractive offer would produce the type of liquidity with which he is more familiar. He would use the sale proceeds to build long-term value for his family and the families of his employees.

In 2015, Gary had five hotels in development that would open the following year. With Madson heading up most of his construction projects, Gary calculated that the company could build six to eight hotels per year. But in typical Gary Tharaldson fashion, once a strategic objective was in sight, it was time to aim higher. Why not double or triple the production rate?

Gary talked with Rick Larson about rejoining him. After the ESOP was created, Larson had worked at TMI as the head of development, which meant he was in charge of constructing the hotels Gary was building from 2006 to 2015. After the ESOP sold, Larson took most of 2015 off and contemplated his future. When Gary contacted him, Larson was open to the idea but said he wanted to establish his own construction company. This made sense since his son, Gregg, was also in the business.

After several meetings, Gary and Larson came to an agreement. They cofounded a company called Dakota Legacy Group (DLG) as a joint venture at the beginning of 2016. And Larson's son serves as a vice president.

On some projects, Gary and Larson each put in 50 percent equity, and the

All Tharaldson Hotels • 1982–2017

Super 8	17	Hilton Garden	2
Choice Comfort Inn	74	Hilton Homewood	17
Choice Econo Lodge	2	IHG Holiday Express	10
Choice Quality Inn	2	IHG Staybridge	7
Marriott Fairfield	129	Carlson Country Inn	14
Marriott Residence	63	Sleep Inn	2
Marriott Courtyard	28	Days Inn	5
Marriott Springhill	7	Best Western	1
Marriott TownePlace	10	LaQuinta	1
Hilton Hampton Inn	36	**Total Built**	**428**

hotel is a partnership from the start. On other projects, Gary hires DLG to complete construction for a fee and a small percentage of the final product.

With Larson on board, Gary is currently ramping up hotel construction to meet a new goal: 100 hotels built or under construction by the end of 2020. As he and Larson planned together, Gary opened five hotels in 2016 and then another four in 2017. He also bought a hotel (a Holiday Inn Express in Las Vegas), which had just opened. Another two hotels were scheduled to open in late 2017, but there have been some construction delays.

And then: boom! With Madson, Jonathan Boyd and Larson all working on Gary's various hotel construction projects, there are 23 hotels in the pipeline for 2018 (plus the two that were scheduled to open in 2017), 22 more for 2019 and one for 2020 with 10 additional hotels in the works. That would bring the total number of hotels to 94. If Gary and company get just six more hotels underway by 2020, the 100-hotel goal will have been reached. If past is prelude, there will likely be about 120 hotels built or in the pipeline by December 31, 2020.

The financial scale of this endeavor is breathtaking. The all-in cost for the 56 hotels currently in development is $1.12 billion, or almost $20 million each. Gary is adhering to his 65-35 debt-to-equity formula in order to avoid becoming overleveraged. Still, that means he is putting up $370 million in

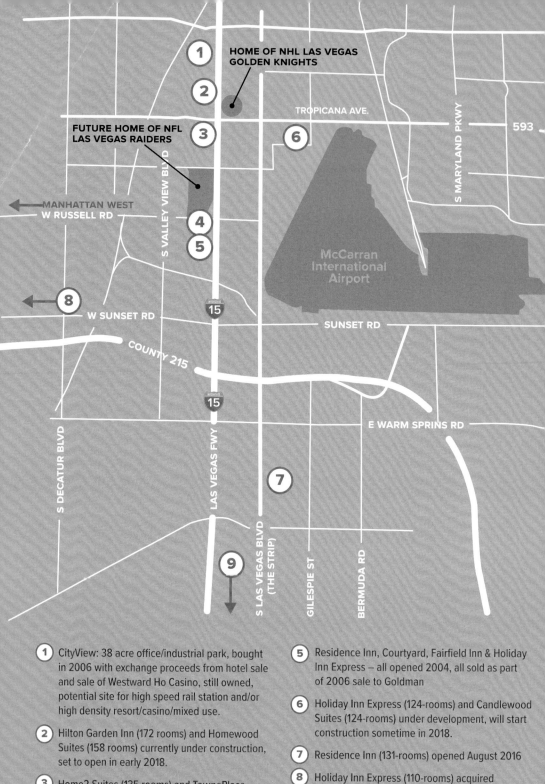

HOME OF NHL LAS VEGAS GOLDEN KNIGHTS

FUTURE HOME OF NFL LAS VEGAS RAIDERS

TROPICANA AVE.

S MARYLAND PKWY

593

S VALLEY VIEW BLVD

MANHATTAN WEST
W RUSSELL RD

McCarran International Airport

15

W SUNSET RD

COUNTY 215

SUNSET RD

15

E WARM SPRINS RD

S DECATUR BLVD

LAS VEGAS FWY

S LAS VEGAS BLVD (THE STRIP)

GILESPIE ST

BERMUDA RD

① CityView: 38 acre office/industrial park, bought in 2006 with exchange proceeds from hotel sale and sale of Westward Ho Casino, still owned, potential site for high speed rail station and/or high density resort/casino/mixed use.

② Hilton Garden Inn (172 rooms) and Homewood Suites (158 rooms) currently under construction, set to open in early 2018.

③ Home2 Suites (135 rooms) and TownePlace Suites (111-rooms) under construction, opening Summer 2018

④ Staybridge Suites (118-rooms), opened 2008.

⑤ Residence Inn, Courtyard, Fairfield Inn & Holiday Inn Express – all opened 2004, all sold as part of 2006 sale to Goldman

⑥ Holiday Inn Express (124-rooms) and Candlewood Suites (124-rooms) under development, will start construction sometime in 2018.

⑦ Residence Inn (131-rooms) opened August 2016

⑧ Holiday Inn Express (110-rooms) acquired March 2017

⑨ Urban Village: 36 acres of vacant land, acquired 50 acres in 2005, sold 14 acres to Centex in 2006.

equity—and that's all cash. Quite a leap in just five years from his dance with bankruptcy.

The hotels range in size from 96 to 172 rooms for a total of 6,290 rooms. The average size is 112 rooms. Land costs are much higher now than for most of Gary's previous hotels, ranging from $1.5 million to $5.45 million.

There are some interesting new developments in this portfolio. For example, the two hotels that were delayed until early 2018 share one site in Las Vegas, as shown in the architectural rendering on page 238. There is a 172-room Hilton Garden Inn and a 158-room Homewood Suites. Both structures are six-stories high, which is new for Gary. Poured concrete is being used to build the bottom floor of each building. Then the top five stories are frame constructions, per usual. Although these are large hotels in Gary's port-folio, they are quite small compared to the major hotels nearby. The Bellagio Hotel, for example, has 3,950 rooms and Caesar's Palace has 3,976 rooms. Together, these two hotels have more rooms than Gary plans to build in the next three years.

Another interesting evolution—or experiment, perhaps—can be seen in the architectural rendering on page 239 of the Residence Inn hotel in a 32-story high-rise building in Grand Rapids, Michigan. The hotel will occupy floors two through 13 and have 130 rooms. There will be luxury condos on the floors above and retail and office space on the floors below the hotel. The start of construction has yet to be determined, but the land has been purchased and the project is under contract.

This is the first building that Gary has commissioned that he is not constructing. The contract involves a set-price with a reputable builder. As well, Gary is partnering with Larson on this project as a joint venture. No doubt Larson will make sure that the hotel is built properly to all specifi-cations.

"If for some reason, this hotel doesn't work out," said Gary, "we can renovate the floors and sell them for condos."

Meanwhile, Fyke continues to make sure that Gary's hotels perform well. The guest satisfaction ratings remain high, and Fyke pushes her managers to improve. Occupancy rates have been impressive, averaging 76.8 percent over the last eight years. Considering that Gary has opened as many hotels as he

An architectural rendering of the Hilton City Center in Las Vegas. The center includes Hilton Garden Inn, a Homewood Suites that share a parking facility.

owned in 2013, this level is outstanding. Occupancy rates at new hotels tend to be about 7 to 10 percent lower for the first six months of operation. The industry average for occupancy ranges from 63 to 65 percent.

High occupancy rates also push up room rates. To date this year, the average daily room rate at Gary's hotels is $132.50.

When Fyke received that phone call from Gary in 2012 when he confessed he might have to declare bankruptcy, as recounted in Chapter Zero, she never doubted that he would find a way to resolve his challenges. It never occurred to her to look for another job. Fyke's faith in Gary was a well-deserved repayment for the faith he had shown in her throughout her career.

More than having confidence in his business acumen, Fyke had faith in the man. "Gary is a life-changer," she said. Fyke recounted how her life had been transformed far beyond her expectations through working for Gary. Like Gary, she performed well at work as she gained responsibility, while also taking the time off work to devote to her husband and four children as they grew up.

Opposite page, an architectural rendering of a Residence Inn that will occupy 12 floors of a 32-story high-rise in downtown Grand Rapids, Michigan.

Fyke also talked about how the ESOP changed lives. After Starwood bought the plan's hotels, there was an 18-month wait period before the employees were paid out. Finally, in August 2016, the money flowed, creating 90 millionaires and hundreds of recipients receiving over $500,000. The lowest paid housekeepers still got more money from the ESOP than they had earned in their careers with TMI.

Many of these recipients expressed their gratitude to Gary in person or in a phone call, and some wrote letters. Carolyn Curran, currently the executive housekeeper at the Courtyard by Marriott in Springfield, Illinois, wrote:

> Gary Tharaldson is an outstanding man. I started with Tharaldson in 2001. I am grateful for the opportunity to be part of his company. Not only did Tharaldson Enterprises help me grow professionally, it helped me save for my family's future because of the employee stock ownership plan. I look back at my years with the company, and I think to myself that if I had to start all over and do it again, I would in a heartbeat. I cannot begin to thank him enough.

Jenny Wilmore started as a receptionist at corporate headquarters in 2005 and then worked in the capital improvements department for Gary and then at TMI. She wrote:

> Being part of the ESOP put me decades ahead in my retirement account. I received a free retirement account without having to contribute my own funds. All I had to do in return was work hard, be part of a team and company I loved, and it would pay me back. I don't think anyone truly understood how big this fund would grow for us. We watched the year-to-year growth, but there was no way of preparing for how profitable this account became for us. It was an unexpected opportunity for my future without knowing much about the ESOP when I started. There is no way that I or anyone else on my level could ever thank Gary enough for giving us the platform we need for retirement.

Wilmore recently rejoined Gary to work at Fargo headquarters on capital improvements for his hotels and other properties. As everyone else who has rejoined Gary in building his third hospitality empire, Wilmore no longer has to work. Gary set her, and especially his top employees, up for a comfortable retirement. Yet, they willingly return to help build his legacy company.

A few months after the ESOP payout, Gary had dinner with his once and perhaps future friend who precipitated the Hans and McKay lawsuits. The friend expressed remorse at his actions and losing control of his emotions. He was also bitterly angry about how his lawyers had tried to take advantage of the situation. The lawsuit he had filed against Gary about their contract dispute was resolved in 2005, and he received no more than he would have without legal action. All for naught.

"I can't hold a grudge," said Gary.

Nor does he like to leave any employees behind. Julie Wrigley works as Fyke's executive secretary and missed out on the ESOP. Nor is she one of the top employees who would normally receive a percentage of one of the hotels as a retirement asset. After hearing often about how valuable Wrigley is to Fyke on a day-to-day basis at her office in Decatur, Gary decided to gift her a small portion of one hotel to fund her retirement dreams. On July 6, 2017, she wrote:

> Hi Gary,
>
> Aimee just went over your very generous gift with me and I just can't put into words how thankful I am!! I AM now and HAVE ALWAYS BEEN over the top proud to be a part of your team! I have been lucky enough to watch your continued success and see you as such a giving and humble man to so many! I love working for you and Aimee, and I could never ask for more! I will forever be grateful for the way you changed my life. Please know that I could never say thank you enough and will never stop working to make you and Aimee proud. Gary, I sincerely thank you from the bottom of my heart!!!
>
> Julie

When Gary gets to 100 or 120 hotels at the end of 2020, he plans to slow down. "Maybe I'll do five or six hotels a year then," he said. "This isn't really work for me. I'm having the time of my life doing what I love to do."

One of Gary's favorite business quotes, by B.C. Forbes, accurately describes how he has tried to run his companies:

> The most successful executives carefully select understudies. They don't strive to do everything themselves. They train and trust others. This leaves them foot-free, mind-free, with time to think. They have time to receive important callers, to pay worthwhile visits. They have time for their families. No matter how able, any employer or executive who insists on running a one-man enterprise courts unhappy circumstances when his powers dwindle.

Gary's generosity is also an act of gratitude for he knows well that he could not have achieved what he did without an able, devoted team and family around him. If one saying echoes through the ages, it is that wisdom begins with gratitude.

"My biggest pleasure has always been to make a difference," Gary said, "not only in the way we build hotels, but more importantly in people's lives. Not only do I create jobs, but my whole philosophy is about how do I make life better for people that work for me. How do I make them wealthy?"

In fact, Gary is currently trying to figure out a way to bring benefit to all his employees, especially as his company expands with more hotels, just as he did with the ESOP. He has some ideas and will be consulting with ESOP experts about how to proceed and avoid another series of opportunistic lawsuits.

To young people preparing in school for a career or just starting out, Gary says, "You can accomplish great things with hard work, common sense and by doing the right thing."

Gary with the 2009 Championship trophies for Gary's 50+ team and his son Matthew's Class B (the top division) team.

ACKNOWLEDGMENTS

I WOULD LIKE TO THANK Gary and Connie Tharaldson and their family for their openness and hospitality throughout the process of writing this book. It was a pleasure to work with Gary on a weekly basis. Not only was he forthcoming about every aspect of his business, but he was also very patient in explaining the complexities of finance, real estate and the hospitality industry. I am also very grateful for the help that Gary's employees offered. Whenever I needed documents, graphics or information, they responded quickly and graciously.

Inspired by Gary's story, University of Mary President Monsignor James Shea and Jerome Richter, the university's Vice President for Mission Advancement and Public Affairs, initiated this project to share with readers the account of Gary's phenomenal career and admirable character, and steadfastly provided the support and resources needed to bring it to completion.

I am most fortunate to have had Jerry Anderson as the book's photographer and art director. His work is superb. Also, I would like to thank and praise Tom Marple's work as illustrator. Fellow writer and editor Karen Herzog contributed expert editing, as did the copy editor, Barbara Spindel. Thanks also to Ashley Theisen, Human Resources Coordinator at the University of Mary, for proofing the manuscript. Several students at the University of Mary—including Sara Duran, Ronita Dutta, Andrea Evinger and Emily Lynse—helped enthusiastically with photocopying, proofing and researching tasks.